D0547496

HE SHINES IN ALL THAT'S FAIR

THE STOB LECTURES 2000

The annual Stob Lectures, normally devoted to the fields of ethics, apologetics, and philosophical theology, are presented each fall on the campus of Calvin College or Calvin Theological Seminary in honor of Henry J. Stob.

Dr. Stob, with degrees from Calvin College and Calvin Theological Seminary, Hartford Seminary, and the University of Göttingen, began his distinguished career as a professor of philosophy at Calvin College in 1939 and in 1952 was appointed to teach philosophical and moral theology at Calvin Theological Seminary, where he remained until retirement. He died in 1996, leaving many students influenced greatly by his teaching.

The Stob Lectures are funded by the Henry J. Stob Endowment and are administered by a committee including the presidents of Calvin College and Calvin Theological Seminary.

For more information on Dr. Stob and The Stob Lectures, see www.calvin.edu/stob.

HE SHINES IN ALL THAT'S FAIR

Culture and Common Grace

• •

THE 2000 STOB LECTURES

Richard J. Mouw

WILLIAM B. EERDMANS PUBLISHING COMPANY
GRAND RAPIDS, MICHIGAN / CAMBRIDGE, U.K.

WITHDRAWN
HIEBERT LIBRARY
FRESNO PACIFIC UNIV.-M. B. SEMINARY
FRESNO, CA 93702

© 2001 Wm. B. Eerdmans Publishing Co.
All rights reserved

Wm. B. Eerdmans Publishing Co.
255 Jefferson Ave. S.E., Grand Rapids, Michigan 49503 /
P.O. Box 163, Cambridge CB3 9PU U.K.

Paperback edition 2002

Printed in the United States of America

06 05 04 03 02   7 6 5 4 3 2

Library of Congress Cataloging-in-Publication Data

He shines in all that's fair: culture and common grace:
the 2000 Stob lectures / Richard J. Mouw.
p.   cm.
Includes bibliographical references.
ISBN 0-8028-2111-1 (pbk: alk. paper)
1. Grace (Theology) 2. Reformed Church — Doctrines.
I. Title: 2000 Stob lectures. II. Title: Stob lectures. III. Title.

BT761.3.M68 2001
230′.57 — dc21

2001040276

www.eerdmans.com

HEKMAN LIBRARY
CALVIN COLLEGE & SEMINARY
GRAND RAPIDS, MICHIGAN

CONTENTS

PREFACE

When I was invited to give the 2000 Stob Lectures, I did not hesitate for a moment to accept the assignment. I admired Henry Stob greatly and learned much from him. To deliver a series of lectures established in his honor is a high privilege.

Nor did I have to think much about what my topic would be. The issues relating to the idea of common grace and the battles that have been waged over those issues have long fascinated me. In a sense, questions about common grace have formed the underlying issues in my own intellectual pilgrimage. And I knew that Henry Stob thought about those questions long and hard as well.

The Reformed Journal editors' meetings over which Henry presided in his study were often extended debates about such matters. For me they were delightfully stimulating seminars in Calvinist thought. As I prepared these lectures, I had no difficulty imagining Stob's responses at almost every point, including not a few likely expressions of genuine disagreement.

But two more public memories of Henry Stob were also vivid for me as I took the opportunity to clarify my thoughts about these matters. One was of the wonderfully lucid lecture on "the antithesis" that he once gave at Calvin College, sponsored by the Philosophy Department — the published version of which I discuss in the following pages. This was Stob at his pedagogical best, making distinctions, clarifying terms, insisting upon nuances. The other memory was of a marvelous sermon that he preached at an evening service of Calvin Christian Reformed Church in Grand Rapids, Michigan. His text was John 3:16, and if I remember correctly, it was a sermon he had preached in that congregation before, which he was now being asked by popular demand to deliver again. I am glad I got to hear it. I do not remember all of its content, but I will never forget the power of Stob's dramatic description of the awful forsakenness experienced by the Son of God as he bore the penalty for our sin at Calvary.

The combination of those two memories, the rigorous insistence on clarity and the passionate proclamation of the love that sent the Savior to the Cross, exemplify for me the kind of Calvinism that Henry Stob stood for. And that kind of Calvinism is also, for me, Christian theology at its best. I have no illusions that the following discussion satisfies such high standards. But it is offered in gratitude for the privilege of having sat at the feet of people like Henry Stob.

The chapters of this book are revisions of my 2000 Stob Lectures, with one exception: I have added the chapter on "infralapsarianism" and "supralapsarianism," which appeared in published form prior to the lecture series in the *Calvin Theological Journal*. These topics provided some of my background thinking for my address to the topic of the lectures. I am convinced that including this chapter serves the cause of the overall discussion.

I am grateful to Calvin College and Calvin Seminary for the invitation to give the Stob Lectures. I am also indebted to Jon Pott, vice president at Eerdmans, for his counsel in preparing this published version. Jon also was a part of the small group that spent many hours in Henry Stob's study at *Reformed Journal* meetings, and our discussions of this project have provided occasions for the two of us to review those memories — not only of intense theological debates, but also of many lighter moments. Our recent conversations have also been tinged with much sadness, however, over the untimely death of our younger *Reformed Journal* colleague and friend, Marlin Van Elderen. Warm memories of his wit and wisdom have also been a part of the writing of these chapters.

Chapter One

THINKING ABOUT COMMONNESS

Like most people raised in North American Protestantism, I was taught songs in my early childhood about the love of Jesus. I can't remember a time when I did not know the words to "Jesus Loves Me" and "Jesus Loves the Little Children." These songs celebrate a divine love that sounds inclusive:

> Red and yellow, black and white,
> They are precious in His sight.
> Jesus loves the little children of the world.

But there is another little song I learned at a very early age in the Dutch Reformed Sunday School I attended:

> One door and only one, and yet its sides are two.
> I'm on the inside, on which side are you?

The love-of-Jesus choruses had their intended effect on me: they assured me that I could be a beneficiary of the Savior's love. But I also understood, even in those early years, the intended teaching of the "One door" song: there are two kinds of people in the world, those who belong to Jesus in a special way and those who do not.

Some are inside the door, others are outside. There is no third group. And the question of which group you belong to is of supreme importance. Again, these basics were clear to me even as a little child. The songs that celebrated the love of Jesus were very important to me, but they never inclined me to become a universalist.

These exclusionary themes were also part of my growing up. I was reared in an evangelical pietist culture, where a premium was placed on being "spiritual." This was the opposite of being "worldly." Our sense of the need to separate ourselves from non-Christian culture was reinforced by a fairly explicit set of rules proscribing those behaviors that were taken to be the most visible signs of worldliness.

While I later came to abandon some of the emphases of this pietism in favor of a spirituality wedded to Reformed theology, I still endorse the basic pietist insistence that the Christian community must be very conscious of the significant ways in which God calls us to stand against the prevailing cultures of our fallen world. It was, after all, one of the apostles, writing under the inspiration of the Spirit — and not just a long line of pietist preachers — who admonished us not to "love the world or the things in the world," since "the love of the Father is not in those who love the world" (I John 2:15-16).

During my college years, I puzzled much over the relationship of Christian commitment to secular thought and the broader patterns of culture. I posed some questions — admittedly in a rather naïve spirit — to a Reformed pastor friend, and he gave me a copy of Cornelius Van Til's booklet *Common Grace*,[1] which I read and re-read eagerly. As Van Til spelled out his own views on the subject by critically contrasting them with the perspectives of figures I was just getting to know — Abraham Kuyper, Herman Hoeksema and others — I was impressed by the importance of this topic and the Calvinist framework within which the issues were formulated.

---

1. Cornelius Van Til, *Common Grace* (Philadelphia: Presbyterian and Reformed Publishing Co., 1954).

In these pages I will reflect on the notion of "common grace," as it has been debated by thinkers in the Calvinist tradition. What is it that Christians can assume they have in common with people who have not experienced the saving grace that draws a sinner into a restored relationship with God? To some degree this question has been raised throughout the larger Calvinist community, but I will focus here on the discussions among Dutch Calvinists, whose arguments have been especially intense — even to the point of splitting churches.

A Broader Interest in Commonness

Before getting into my discussion of the ways in which Calvinists have argued with each other about these matters, I want to note that the underlying issues here are of broad contemporary Christian concern. The question of "commonness" actually looms fairly large in theological discussion these days, at various points on the theological spectrum. And what makes the present treatments of the topic especially interesting, particularly in the Protestant world, is that a kind of role reversal has been taking place in the way the topic is being treated. Some of those who in the past were strong defenders of difference are now exploring theologies of commonness, and others who in the past were strong defenders of commonness are now exploring theologies of difference.

Consider the evangelical world. The cultural self-understanding of many evangelical Christians has often been shaped in the past by three closely related pietist motifs: a remnant view of the church, in which Christians saw themselves as inevitably a "little flock" in the midst of a world hostile to the faith; an ethic of "over-againstness," whereby believers were encouraged to establish patterns of living that underscored their separation from the dominant cultural patterns; and a pessimistic, even apocalyptic, assessment of the future course of history. Evangelical groups that have featured these motifs in the past are now moving in a quite different theological direction. They are building mega-churches and strategizing about how to win the "culture wars." Some of them, not too long ago, even chose to describe themselves as representing a new "moral majority" in American life. In these and other ways, commonness themes have come to have a new currency among evangelicals over the past few decades.

A very different tendency can be discerned within segments of mainstream Protestantism, where some thinkers are intentionally downplaying commonness. In the recent book *Good News in Exile: Three Pastors Offer a Hopeful Vision for the Church*, the authors, each of them a pastor in a mainline denomination, tell of their theological pilgrimages away from the strong emphasis on a continuity between the gospel and culture that they had learned from their liberal Protestant mentors. Martin Copenhaver's story is a good case in point. The senior pastor of Wellesley Congregational Church in Massachusetts, Copenhaver describes himself as "a child of American liberal Protestantism." The understanding of the gospel that Copenhaver grew up with is nicely captured, he reports, in a characterization of liberal preaching offered by an atheist friend of his: "You hear what the psychologist says, what the historian says, what *The New York Times* editorial writer says, and then the sermon concludes with, 'And perhaps Jesus said it best. . . .'" But now Copenhaver preaches a very different message, one that stands over against the "accumulated wisdom of humankind." Instead of "perhaps Jesus said it best," he senses an obligation to proclaim, "You have heard it said . . . but Jesus says to you . . . ."[2]

William Willimon, the well-known dean of the chapel at Duke University, presents a similar case. Willimon hammers away at what he sees as the mistaken emphasis on continuity in mainline Protes-

2. Martin B. Copenhaver, Anthony B. Robinson, and William H. Willimon, *Good News in Exile: Three Pastors Offer a Hopeful Vision for the Church* (Grand Rapids: Eerdmans, 1999), pp. 9-11.

4

tantism. For example, he takes on the liberal Episcopal bishop John Shelby Spong for asking how any thoughtful person can expect Spong's physicist daughter to believe in a bodily resurrection: "The answer, I suppose," says Willimon, "depends on Spong's daughter. . . . How little imagination does his daughter now have? . . . The text cannot be blamed if modern people . . . live by epistemologies too limited to enable them to hear the text." We cannot expect people to hear the gospel, Willimon argues, when they are "epistemologically enslaved."[3]

Sometimes Willimon seems to be emphasizing the ways in which entrapment in the particular thought patterns of "modernity" limits people's capacity to understand the gospel. But it is clear that he and his colleagues also sense a more general epistemological problem. When people can't hear the message of Christ, that message "itself shares some of the 'blame' . . . contending, as the gospel does, that the solution to what ails us lies somewhere out beyond ourselves."[4] It is not enough, they insist, to think about the gospel's "solution" without also thinking about how Christ redefines the problems for which his transforming power is the remedy.

Looking for Commonness

It is encouraging to see within mainline Protestantism this insightful critique of the older liberal optimism about the potentials of an unfettered human spirit. Calvinists who have long insisted on the reality of the antithesis between Christian and non-Christian patterns of life and thought should be especially gratified by the appearance of such antitheticalist motifs. And while I worry that the contrast made by these critics between redeemed and non-redeemed con-

3. Erskine Clarke, ed., *Exilic Preaching: Testimony for Christian Exiles in an Increasingly Hostile Culture* (Harrisburg, Pa.: Trinity Press International, 1998), pp. 110, 130.

4. Clarke, *Exilic Preaching*, p. 134.

sciousness is put too starkly, I do think that we do well to learn from their warnings, even as I believe that we also have much to learn from people within the Calvinist ranks who place a strong and uncompromising emphasis on "difference."

For all that, however, I am still convinced — and this will be clear in what follows — that we need to search for the proper grounds of commonness. But it is important to search carefully. On what basis do we posit a commonality between those who have put their faith in Jesus Christ and those who have not done so? This question has particular importance as we try to articulate a biblical perspective for Christian involvement in public life in our contemporary context. Our present cultural situation requires some new formulations regarding human commonness. In past eras our Christian theologies of commonness were motivated in part by a desire — indeed, a sense of obligation — to provide alternatives to influential non-Christian systems of thought where an emphasis on human commonness loomed large. Augustine, for example, agreed with the Platonists that a rational "light" illuminates the minds of all human beings; but, he insisted, the Platonist explanations for this phenomenon were inadequate because they did not acknowledge the ministry of the "the true light which enlightens everyone" (John 1:9), the One whose glory we have beheld in the person of Jesus Christ. Similarly, Thomas Aquinas saw himself as building upon, but also as correcting, Aristotle's account of our shared human potentials. And many Christians in the modern era were eager to provide a biblical basis for acknowledging the universal rationality that featured so prominently in various Enlightenment portrayals of the human condition.

Today, however, Christian discussions of commonness take on a somewhat different tone, because of a widespread emphasis on *un*commonness. This is all too apparent, not only in the very visible tribal and ethnic conflicts that now disrupt life in so many places in the world, but also in some patterns of intellectual life, where prominent thinkers are attacking the very idea of a "meta-narrative." They insist that there is no legitimate way of articulating a basis for our common humanness, because every such formulation is oppressive. In this line of thinking, the attempt to group all human beings under a common "story" is in fact nothing more than a brutal exercise of power, in which some groups exercise hegemonic control over others. As the self-described "postmodern" thinker Iban Hassan puts the case, we are living in "an antinomian moment" in which we must all recognize the need to "unmake" and "deconstruct" all "totalizing" accounts of the human condition. What this rejection of "the tyranny of wholes" means, he says, is that we must live with "an epistemological obsession with fragments."[5]

In such a climate, our search for the grounds of commonness must be motivated by a faith that cuts against the grain of much of contemporary life and thought. But it is not enough simply to affirm commonness. This is an important time to explore the underlying Christian foundations for an understanding of what we hold in common with those who reject the biblical message. The Christian tradition offers many significant resources on the topic of commonness, and many of these resources are now being explored anew as Christian thinkers have begun to worry about the cultural impact of the relativism that accompanies the current fascination with deep differences. One obvious place to look is the "natural law" tradition, and it is gratifying to see how Christians from several traditions — particularly Roman Catholics and evangelicals — are engaged in dialogue about how natural law themes can be appropriated for our contemporary context.[6]

5. Quoted in Richard Bernstein, *The New Constellation: The Ethical-Political Horizons of Modernity/Postmodernity* (Boston: MIT Press, 1992), p. 199.

6. See, for example, the essays and dialogues in Michael Cromartie, ed., *Preserving Grace: Protestants, Catholics and Natural Law* (Grand Rapids: Eerdmans, 1997). A more systematic treatment is given by the Roman Catholic ethicist Jean Porter, in her book *Natural and Divine Law: Reclaiming the Tradition for Christian Ethics* (Grand Rapids: Eerdmans, 1999), which includes a sympathetic foreword by the Reformed philosopher Nicholas Wolterstorff.

The discussion that follows here is presented in the conviction that Calvinist discussions of the idea of common grace are an important resource for addressing the contemporary issues of commonness and difference. While I do not think that we need to choose between, say, natural law and common grace, I do see these discussions of common grace as embodying sensitivities — ones that I take seriously as a Calvinist — that are not present in other ways of addressing the issues. I am also convinced that much important content in these Calvinist debates has been hidden too long from the larger Christian theological world. My efforts here, then, are an attempt to give Dutch Reformed deliberations about common grace some broader ecumenical exposure.

Chapter Two

LESSONS FROM THE "LABADISTS"

In the 1920s, the question of commonness was debated intensely — indeed, angrily, and with divisive results — within the Christian Reformed Church. By that time most of the intellectual establishment in that Dutch-American Calvinist denomination had been strongly influenced by the idea, developed at length by several theologians in the Netherlands, that, in addition to the saving grace imparted only to the elect, God shows a *common* grace to humankind in general. However, Herman Hoeksema, a prominent pastor-theologian in Grand Rapids, Michigan, took exception to this idea. Hoeksema made his case forcefully, and in much detail, but his views were not welcomed by the majority. In 1924, the church's synod issued an official declaration on the subject, insisting that there is indeed a kind of non-salvific attitude of divine favor toward all human beings, manifested in three ways: (1) the bestowal of natural gifts, such as rain and sunshine, upon creatures in general, (2) the restraining of sin in human affairs, so that the unredeemed do not produce all of the evil that their depraved natures might otherwise bring about, and (3) the ability of unbelievers to perform acts of civic good. Hoeksema's refusal to submit to these teachings prompted his departure, along with several congregations and pastors who supported his cause, from the Christian Reformed

9

Church. Together they established the Protestant Reformed Churches in 1925.[1]

Over three quarters of a century have passed since that controversy raged among the Dutch Calvinists, and the specifics of the debates have largely been forgotten — except within the membership of the Protestant Reformed denomination, where the doctrine of common grace is still being criticized.[2] Nevertheless, the underlying issues are still important ones. For those of us who consider ourselves to be in the "mainstream" of Calvinist thought, it is a helpful exercise, I think, to look back on the debates of the 1920s to see what relevance they might have for our current efforts to understand the church's relationship to the broader culture.

New Social Conditions

It is also helpful, however, to be clear about how our present situation differs from the conditions that gave rise to the older controversies. James Bratt has convincingly argued that the debates of the 1920s arose in the context of what he labels "the decisive decade of Americanization" for Midwestern Dutch-American Calvinists.[3] The

1. For the complete text of the "Three Points" of 1924, see Herman Hoeksema, *The Protestant Reformed Churches in America: Their Origin, Early History and Doctrine* (Grand Rapids: First Protestant Reformed Church, 1936), pp. 84-85. Hoeksema's book also provides the texts of other relevant documents and gives the most detailed account of the events surrounding the official proceedings, as well as his interpretation of the ecclesiastical and theological issues at stake.

2. See, for example, Herman Hanko, *For Thy Truth's Sake: A Doctrinal History of the Protestant Reformed Churches* (Grandville, Mich.: Reformed Free Publishing Association, 2000), a volume published on the occasion of the seventh-fifth anniversary of the Protestant Reformed Churches.

3. James D. Bratt, *Dutch Calvinism in Modern America: A History of a Conservative Subculture* (Grand Rapids: Eerdmans, 1984), pp. 105-19; the "decisive decade of Americanization" comment is on p. 119.

Dutch-Americans, many of whom were first- or second-generation immigrants, were gradually opening up to the larger culture. As American ways were becoming more familiar, fellow citizens in the broader society did not seem as "other" as they had before. For many Dutch-Americans, the question of "commonness" as it was posed in the common grace discussion had a positive tone: how could they explain the similarities that they were discovering as they got to know their non-Dutch neighbors better? I do not mean to reduce the theological issues involved to purely sociological ones, but simply to recognize the social context in which the theological debates took on a sense of existential poignancy.

For those of us today who still see common grace as an important theological topic, the issue of Americanization is no longer a significant factor in the discussion. Dutch-American Calvinists and other evangelicals who saw themselves as living on the margins of the dominant culture a few generations ago are no longer in a position to debate *whether* to assimilate more. That dominant culture has infiltrated our lives through new technologies and social mobility to such an extent that our conversations about common grace are now perhaps better framed this way: to what degree has the commonness that we *have* embraced in the culture that we share with our non-Christian neighbors compromised our commitment to the gospel?

The Intellectual Climate

It is also important to keep in mind that the earlier debates about common grace took place at a time when Enlightenment thought dominated the intellectual orthodoxy of the larger culture. The Dutch Calvinists who argued with each other were well aware of this fact. Given their Calvinist commitments, the Enlightenment idea that all human beings are ultimately accountable to a "neutral" universalizing rationality was repugnant both to those who argued for common grace and to those who argued against it. Writing some sixty years after the conflict, Henry Stob made a point of highlighting the non-neutrality of our cognitive capacities. "The point of view from which the world is surveyed," said Stob, "is not theoretically determined: it is chosen," and "the choice reflects a religious decision. It is an act of faith." This means, Stob insisted, that the redeemed and the unredeemed "view, interpret, and understand the world in radically different ways," and the opposition "extends deep into the intellectual realm and significantly affects all theory."[4] Still, the doctrine of common grace did allow its defenders to find some positive points of contact with secular thought; Stob made his point about non-neutrality only after he had invoked the doctrine of common grace to allow for a created "solidarity of human kind [that] extends also into the realm of the mind, where a shared reason makes it possible for Christians and non-Christians to engage each other in intelligible address, and to conduct meaningful dialogues and debates."[5]

Looking back on these comments from our present intellectual context — even from the short distance of two decades after Stob wrote on the subject — we are aware that talk of a common rationality does not come as easily from many of our secularist contemporaries. It is the emphasis on deep differences that has the more familiar ring today. In our postmodern climate, thinkers like to celebrate the demise of "the Enlightenment project," arguing instead for the "incommensurability" of diverse worldviews and the absence of any "universalizing meta-narrative" — and insisting that all reasoning is guided by non-rational factors. Thus, a Calvinist who emphasizes human solidarity and a shared rationality in this present context goes against the grain of some widely held perspectives in contempo-

4. Henry Stob, "Observations on the Concept of the Antithesis," in Peter De Klerk and Richard R. De Ridder, eds., *Perspectives on the Christian Reformed Church: Studies in Its History, Theology, and Ecumenicity* (Grand Rapids: Baker Book House, 1983), pp. 252-53.

5. Stob, "Observations," pp. 248-49.

rary thought. Given the present state of cultural confusion, this change may itself provide sufficient motivation for a re-examination of common grace theology.

Exploring a Mystery

Professor Foppe Ten Hoor, a theologian and elder statesman in the Christian Reformed Church during the common grace controversy of the 1920s, was never one to avoid a good theological debate, but he was reluctant to join the fray on common grace. According to one account, Professor Ten Hoor publicly stated "that he had studied the problem for forty years, that he felt quite sure that there was such a thing as common grace, but that he did not know what it was!" The reporter here was Herman Hoeksema,[6] who obviously took Ten Hoor's statement to be an expression of theological confusion. I want to offer a different assessment. I think Ten Hoor was offering a profound perspective on the subject of common grace.

Like Professor Ten Hoor, I have been thinking about this subject now for about four decades, and I have ended up pretty much where he did. I am convinced that there is such a thing as common grace, but I am not very clear about what it is. Nor am I embarrassed to admit my relative ignorance. We stand here, I am convinced, before a mystery. But the workings of *special* grace are enshrouded in mystery as well, as our Lord reminded Nicodemus: "The wind blows where it chooses, and you hear the sound of it, but you do not know where it comes from or where it goes. So it is with everyone who is born of the Spirit" (John 3:8).

Still, the shroud of mystery over the operations of grace does not justify a simple retreat into agnosticism. While God's saving ways are in the final analysis unsearchable, that does not mean that we should refuse to get clear about at least some of our thoughts on the

6. Hoeksema, *Protestant Reformed Churches*, p. 67.

subject. We certainly can know enough to be able to challenge viewpoints that seem clearly confused. We can explore the mystery of common grace in that same spirit.

The debates over common grace have covered some rather complex issues, and I will not examine the whole territory here. My specific focus will be on the relevance of teachings about common grace for our understanding of *culture* in our contemporary context. Is there a non-saving grace that is at work in the broader reaches of human cultural interaction, a grace that expedites a desire on God's part to bestow certain blessings on all human beings, elect and non-elect alike — blessings that provide the basis for Christians to cooperate with, and learn from, non-Christians?

While my own sympathies lie with the common grace defenders, I do think that that there are good reasons to pay close attention to the concerns expressed by the dissenters. Indeed, I am convinced that if we are to use common grace motifs in a healthy manner, we will need regularly to test our thoughts and practices against the challenges posed by those Christians who are critical of the way those motifs have been defended. In what follows, then, I will attempt to give careful attention to those dissenting views.

The Antithesis and "the Natural Mind"

Calvinists have typically discussed common grace in connection with the idea of *the antithesis,* a theological notion that is seen by thinkers on both sides of the debates as standing in tension with an emphasis on common grace. For the dissenters, the very fact of the tension means that common grace thinking must be rejected. The defenders argue, on the other hand, that the tension must be recognized and embraced.

The term *antithesis,* as Henry Stob observed in his helpful essay on the topic, is "derived from *anti* (against) and *tithemi* (to set)," and is meant to depict "two entities, moments, or principles that are set over against each other."[7] The term gained philosophical currency in the writings of Kant and Hegel, but it was enlisted for a special theological use by the Dutch "neo-Calvinist" thinkers of the nineteenth century. Abraham Kuyper and others referred frequently to *the* antithesis, by which they meant the radical opposition that characterizes, in Stob's words, the "real and uncompromising, although uneven, contest being waged between God and Satan, between Christ and antichrist, between the seed of the woman and the seed of the serpent, between the church and the world."[8]

Of course, the *idea* of the antithesis was present in Calvinist thought from the beginning. John Calvin himself even used the term in a way that anticipated the more technical sense later developed in nineteenth-century Dutch Calvinism. When a person is converted, Calvin argued, God graciously transforms "an evil will to a good will." Thus, "the new creation . . . sweeps away everything of our common [depraved] nature." This transforming action is required, Calvin observed as he explained Paul's line of reasoning in Ephesians 2, because of "an antithesis between Adam and Christ."[9]

John Calvin's views on the capacity of the unregenerate mind to discover truth and goodness have been much debated. It is certainly possible to find comments in his writings that could encourage the development of a doctrine of common grace. For one thing, Calvin is convinced that radical sinfulness would quickly lead to ruin if not held back by divine restraint. God, he tells us, keeps the depraved strivings of unredeemed human beings in check "by throwing a bridle over them . . . that they may not break loose," especially when the Lord deems doing so "to be expedient to preserve all that is."[10] But Calvin also uses more positive terms to describe the capacities of fallen humanity. Sin does not destroy our shared social nature, for

7. Stob, "Observations," p. 241.

8. Stob, "Observations," p. 242.

9. John Calvin, *Institutes of the Christian Religion,* ed. John T. McNeill, trans. Ford Lewis Battles (Philadelphia: Westminster Press, 1960), II.3.6, pp. 297-98.

10. Calvin, *Institutes* II.3.3, p. 292.

"there exist in all men's minds universal impressions of a certain civic fair dealing and order. Hence no man is to be found who does not understand that every sort of human organization must be regulated by laws, and who does not comprehend the principles of those laws."[11]

Calvin's own legal studies had focused on the writings of ancient Roman jurists and rhetoricians, especially Seneca, and he was clearly conscious of his intellectual debt to these pagan thinkers. There is, says Calvin, "a universal apprehension of reason and understanding [that] is by nature implanted in men," which, "because it is bestowed indiscriminately upon pious and impious, . . . is rightly counted among natural gifts." Indeed, he insists, every human being ought to recognize this implanted rational nature as a "peculiar grace of God."[12] And when we observe this gift at work in "secular writers," Calvin advises, we should

> let that admirable light of truth shining in them teach us that the mind of man, though fallen and perverted from its wholeness, is nevertheless clothed and ornamented with God's excellent gifts. If we regard the Spirit of God as the sole fountain of truth, we shall neither reject the truth itself, nor despise it where it shall appear, unless we wish to dishonor the Spirit of God. . . . Those men whom Scripture [I Cor. 2:14] calls "natural men" were, indeed, sharp and penetrating in their investigation of inferior things. Let us, accordingly, learn by their example how many gifts the Lord left to human nature even after it was despoiled of its true good.[13]

Again, it is easy to see how defenders of the doctrine of common grace would later seize upon passages like these. Indeed, given Calvin's comments here about the capabilities of "natural men" — almost celebratory in tone — we might be tempted to ask how anyone

11. Calvin, *Institutes* II.2.13, p. 272.
12. Calvin, *Institutes* II.2.14, p. 273.
13. Calvin, *Institutes* II.2.15, pp. 273-75.

in the Calvinist tradition could insist on a pessimistic assessment. However, Calvin himself provides other statements that demonstrate less optimism about what the unredeemed mind is capable of producing. When, in the passage on the subject quoted above, Calvin credits the unredeemed with some grasp of the principles of civic fairness, he quickly adds a caveat regarding "the dissensions and conflicts" that regularly attend "natural" social relationships. Even when the human mind "seems to follow the way," he observes, inevitably "it limps and staggers."[14] And while Calvin does acknowledge that "God, in providing for the human race, often endows with a heroic nature those destined to command" — thus producing "the qualities of great leaders celebrated in histories" — Calvin goes on to observe that because these leaders are motivated by their own ambition, their "virtues are so sullied that before God they lose all favor," so that anything in them "that appears praiseworthy must be considered worthless."[15]

Similarly, Calvin does not let his positive comments about the specifically intellectual virtues of the unredeemed go unqualified. While it is true that "in man's perverted and degenerate nature some sparks still gleam," he says, the light is nonetheless "choked with dense ignorance, so that it cannot come forth effectively." The fallen "mind, because of its dullness, cannot hold to the right path, but wanders through various errors and stumbles repeatedly, as if it were groping in the darkness. . . . Thus it betrays how incapable it is of seeking and finding truth."[16] The Synod of Dordtrecht nicely captured the nuances of Calvin's overall assessment in its article on "The Inadequacy of the Light of Nature":

> There remain, however, in man since the fall, the glimmerings of natural light, whereby he retains some knowledge of God, of natural things, and the difference between good and evil, and discovers

14. Calvin, *Institutes* II.2.13, pp. 272-73.
15. Calvin, *Institutes* II.3.4, p. 294.
16. Calvin, *Institutes* II.2.12, pp. 270-71.

17

some regard for virtue, good order in society, and for maintaining an orderly external deportment. But so far is this light of nature from being sufficient to bring him to a saving knowledge of God, and to true conversion, that he is incapable of using it aright even in things natural and civil. Nay farther, this light, such as it is, man in various ways renders wholly polluted, and holds it [back] in unrighteousness; by doing which he becomes inexcusable before God.[17]

The opponents of common grace teachings, then, do not simply disagree with Calvin. They may wish that he had chosen his words differently at a few points, as when, for example, he describes God's indiscriminate distribution of rational insight to the "pious and impious" alike as an operation of "peculiar grace." But they can legitimately claim nonetheless to be working within the general contours of Calvin's thought.

Against Common Grace

A basic concern underlying all of the specific criticisms set forth by the opponents of common grace teaching has to do with the use of idea of *grace* in this context. As Hoeksema points out, the elect experience many evils in their lives, such as sickness, grief and poverty; but surely these things are not to be taken as visitations of divine *wrath* on the godly. Why, then, Hoeksema asks, should we take the *good* things that visit the lives of the *un*godly as evidence of grace?[18] He believed that viewing the non-elect as somehow benefiting from the restraint of sin, or from rain and sunshine that nurture the crops of the elect and the non-elect alike, is a lot like using the term "blessing" to describe the experience of someone who is enjoying "a nice

17. The Canons of the Synod of Dort, Heads III and IV, art. 4, in Philip Schaff, ed., *The Creeds of Christendom, with a History and Critical Notes,* vol. III (Grand Rapids: Baker Books, 1996), p. 588.

18. Hoeksema, *Protestant Reformed Churches,* p. 313.

sleigh-ride on a beautifully smooth and slippery road that ends in a deep precipice." How, he asks, can we attribute to "grace" something that leads to the recipient's "inevitable destruction"?[19]

What the common grace doctrine attributes to divine favor, its critics see as wholly explainable in terms of the workings of providence. While they concede that there are indeed important ways in which depraved people fit into God's good purposes for the creation, they do not believe this justifies our thinking of the non-elect as receiving some sort of blessing from God, or of God working "internally" in their souls to make them less depraved. According to Hoeksema,

> [T]he natural man, . . . both with relation to all created things on the one hand and to God on the other, cannot, will not and cannot will to do the will of God. He is still prophet, priest and king, but of the devil and in covenant with him. And while God in his providence and by the Word of His power sustains his nature as man, and sustains his relation to the universe, thus providing him with means to develop and realize his life in the organism of all things, with these things man is always the sinner, the ungodly, the object of the wrath of God, gathering for himself treasures of wrath in the day of final judgment.[20]

On the topic of the unredeemed being able to discern and perform acts of civic good, Hoeksema acknowledges that the non-elect do have a grasp of the principles that are necessary for proper societal living. But since such a person "does not seek after God, nor aim at Him and His glory," the actual result of all of this is that he uses his social efforts to rebel against God, leading also to "evil effects upon himself and his fellow creatures."[21] We must not think of the capacity to work for civic good as resulting from an "internal" work

19. Hoeksema, *Protestant Reformed Churches*, p. 314.
20. Hoeksema, *Protestant Reformed Churches*, p. 307.
21. Hoeksema, *Protestant Reformed Churches*, p. 372.

of the Spirit that modifies the depraved nature by injecting virtuous intentions into the reprobate's inner life: "though there is some regard for virtue and good order and orderly external deportment, . . . inwardly he is not virtuous at all, but even in this regard for virtue [he is] a seeker of self . . . [who] does not love God, neither God's precepts, but seeks to maintain himself."[22]

The Threat of "Labadism"

The passion with which many of the defenders of common grace have rejected the views of Hoeksema and other critics of their position is on the face of it somewhat puzzling. Why has this particular issue been such a divisive one? One is tempted to look beyond the theological issues themselves to other sorts of explanatory factors. James Bratt did this quite successfully, I judge, in exploring the ways the Christian Reformed controversies of the 1920s can be examined in light of the Americanization process. We can probably also see something of what Freudians call "the narcissism of minor differences," in which two individuals or groups are so close to each other that small differences between them become very large in their imaginations. But I am convinced that these extra-theological insights do not fully explain the passion that is aroused in these discussions. We must do some further *theological* probing.

An important clue can be found, I suggest, in the rhetoric that the common grace defenders use in dealing with their critics. Hoeksema gives a poignant example of this rhetoric as he remembers with bitterness how his opponents characterized his theological perspective during the controversies of the 1920s: "all that opposed them and refused to believe and proclaim this theory of common grace, they proudly and disdainfully branded as Anabaptist!"[23] This

22. Hoeksema, *Protestant Reformed Churches*, p. 384.
23. Hoeksema, *Protestant Reformed Churches*, p. 16.

tactic has been common in the Calvinist tradition. When the going gets tough in an intra-Reformed controversy, there frequently comes a point when one of the parties reaches into the rhetorical arsenal and employs what seems for all the world to be one of the worst insults one Calvinist can toss at another: they call their opponent an Anabaptist.

From the time of the Reformation onward Calvinist thinkers have been eager to portray Anabaptist thought as dangerous and unworthy of serious theological engagement. A good case in point is Article 36 of the 1561 Belgic Confession, where the Reformed churches proclaim that they "detest the error of the Anabaptists and other seditious people" for the way in which they "reject the higher powers and magistrates, and would subvert justice, introduce a community of goods."[24] They could say this even though the Anabaptists had already been on record for over three decades, in the Schleitheim Confession of 1527, as affirming that the exercise of the sword is indeed "ordained of God" — albeit "outside the perfection of Christ" — in that it "punishes and puts to death the wicked, and guards and protects the good," and is now "ordained to be used by the worldly magistrates."[25]

Willem Balke's detailed account of John Calvin's many disputes with the Anabaptists[26] provides much evidence that Calvin's own frustrations with the Anabaptists had to do with the fact that the Anabaptists "out-Calvinisted" the Reformed community on at least two important points. The first was church discipline. The Calvinists were quite critical of Catholics and Lutherans for their lack of attention to the role of discipline in the Christian community, but the Anabaptists took discipline even further than the Calvinists, insisting on even tighter patterns of communal control. The Calvinists responded by condemning the Anabaptists for demanding, in Calvin's

---

24. Belgic Confession, Art. XXXVI, in Schaff, *Creeds,* Vol. III, p. 433.

25. The Schleitheim Confession, Art. VI, http://www.anabaptists.org/history/schleith.html

26. Willem Balke, *Calvin and the Anabaptist Radicals,* trans. William Heynen (Grand Rapids: Eerdmans, 1981).

words, "angelic perfection."[27] The second point had to do with the relationship of the church to the world. Calvinism, having begun its depiction of the human condition with a stark portrayal of human depravity, regularly introduced the sorts of modifications — which would later show up in the form of a full-blown common grace theology — that allowed Calvinists to endorse some of the things going on in the larger culture, especially the workings of civil government. On this point the Anabaptists accused them of inconsistency, insisting that a negative assessment of unregenerate human nature required a strict posture of separation from the world. Here the Calvinist response featured the kind of condemnatory language we saw in the Belgic Confession.

Several years ago John Howard Yoder and I joined forces from both sides of the Reformed-Anabaptist divide to argue that the disagreements between Calvinists and Anabaptists should not be construed as disputes between radically different theological types, but instead as a family argument. The high intensity of these disputes, we concurred, is due to the fact that the differences between the two groups are of a more intimate character than are either of their arguments with, say, Lutherans or Catholics. This is because Anabaptist thought is, in effect, a radicalization of some key Calvinist themes.[28] It should not surprise us, then, that some of the most passionate debates within the Reformed community have addressed an agenda similar to the Reformed-Anabaptist arguments.

The term "Labadist" is another label of contempt used by Calvinists to refer to what they see as Anabaptist-type tendencies *within* the Calvinist camp. It derives from the teachings of Jean de Labadie, a seventeenth-century Jesuit who converted to Calvinism and served for a while as a pastor of a Dutch Reformed congregation. Labadie encouraged the formation of intimate fellowship groups *(gezelschappen)* as a

27. Calvin, *Institutes* IV.12.12, p. 1239.
28. Cf. John H. Yoder, "Reformed Versus Anabaptist Social Strategies: An Inadequate Typology" and Richard J. Mouw, "Abandoning the Typology: A Reformed Assist," *TSF Bulletin* 8, no. 5 (May-June 1985): 2-10.

supplement to more formal worship services. Eventually, though, these groups became an independent network of house churches led by Labadie, who issued harsh criticisms of the "worldliness" of the larger Reformed body. "Labadist" became, like "Anabaptist," a term of reproach for any group that wanted too much "perfection" in the church and urged too much separation from the world.[29]

As the Christian Reformed pastor-theologian Leonard Verduin has argued in a number of his writings, it is no accident that Anabaptist-type themes keep making their presence known within the Calvinist community.[30] They are not alien thoughts that keep forcing their way in from the outside; they emerge from home-grown convictions. Calvin Seminary professor William Heyns made a similar point — albeit without Verduin's Anabaptist sympathies — in a 1922 letter to Christian Reformed minister J. K. Van Baalen, who had just written a rather inflammatory pamphlet depicting Hoeksema and his associates as Anabaptists. Heyns endorsed the general thrust of Van Baalen's critique, but he chided him for his rhetoric, instructing Van Baalen that he "would have done better to leave out that epithet 'Anabaptist,' which here can serve only as a scornful word." Surely, Heyns wrote, Van Baalen was not ignorant of the fact "that all of the same things" he found in Hoeksema's thinking could "also be said of the old theologians of Reformed scholasticism."[31]

29. Cf. F. Ernest Stoeffler, *The Rise of Evangelical Pietism*, Studies in the History of Religions, vol. 9 (Leiden: E. J. Brill, 1965), pp. 162-69. For examples of accusations of Labadism among the Dutch Reformed in North America, see James Tanis, *Dutch Calvinist Pietism in the Middle Colonies: A Study in the Life and Theology of Theodorus Jacobus Frelinghuysen* (The Hague: Martinus Nijhoff, 1967), pp. 143-45, 151, 159; and William O. Van Eyck, *Landmarks of the Reformed Fathers, or What Dr. Van Raalte's People Believed* (Grand Rapids: Reformed Press, 1922), pp. 189, 196.

30. See, for example, Leonard Verduin, *Honor Your Mother: Christian Reformed Roots in the 1834 Separation* (Grand Rapids, Mich.: CRC Publications, 1988), p. 21.

31. Letter from W. Heyns to J. K. Van Baalen, Nov. 3, 1922, Heritage Hall, Calvin College; translation by Dirk Mouw.

These observations are important for our discussion of common grace. If the Anabaptists deserve more respect than they have typically received from Calvinists, then the Labadists should not have been condemned simply because they resembled Anabaptists. Furthermore, the more recent Calvinist critics of common grace should not be dismissed simply on the grounds that their objections have similarities to the views of Anabaptists and Labadists.

The Antithetical Relationship

At the heart of Herman Hoeksema's sustained critique of common grace theology lies a very practical concern about the life of the church. The commonality emphasis in common grace theology, Hoeksema insists, will inevitably result in the "obliteration of the distinction between the Church and the world, light and darkness, Christ and Belial, righteousness and unrighteousness."[32] Of course, no common grace defender would simply advocate the "obliteration" of the distinctions listed by Hoeksema. But it does seem to be essential to common grace thinking that the distinction between "church and world" is not exactly the same distinction as that which holds between "light and darkness, Christ and Belial, righteousness and unrighteousness."

As Henry Stob explains the notion of the antithesis, for example, he rejects the idea that the antithetical relationship holds between specific classes of people as such: elect and reprobate, regenerate and unregenerate, believer and unbeliever. "The fact is," says Stob, "that the antithesis, at bottom, is between sin and grace."[33] And since the struggle with sin "takes place also within the Christian himself,"[34] and since common grace is at work beyond the

---

32. Hoeksema, *Protestant Reformed Churches,* p. 92.
33. Stob, "Observations," p. 251.
34. Stob, "Observations," p. 246.

walls of the church,[35] the antithesis is not an opposition that holds between the church and the world as such, but between the cause of God and the cause of Satan, each of which can be seen at work in the lives of Christians and non-Christians alike.

Herman Dooyeweerd defended a similar view of the antithesis in a very concrete situation in the Netherlands during the 1940s. The experiences of the Second World War had had a profound impact on many orthodox Calvinists who had previously emphasized a strict sense of separation from the world. However, the shared experience of standing against a common foe with people of different religious and non-religious beliefs during the horrors of the Nazi occupation stirred up feelings of social solidarity that did not simply disappear when the war ended. The result was the formation of the Dutch National Movement *(Nederlandse Volksbeweging),* an organization that issued a manifesto stating that, given the need to form "[t]he greatest possible consensus among the various religious and political groups" for postwar Dutch life, it was clear that both "the Christian antithesis and the Marxist class struggle are no longer fruitful principles for the solution of today's social problems."[36] Dooyeweerd was distressed by this development, and he responded with a series of articles in which he defended at length the idea of the antithesis. Early on in his discussion he too addresses the question of what the antithesis is *between.* Like Stob, he is reluctant to see it as an opposition between identifiable groups of human beings. The antithesis, he insists, should not be thought of as "a dividing line between Christian and non-Christian groups. It is the unrelenting battle between two spiritual principles that cut through the nation and through all mankind."[37]

I think Stob and Dooyeweerd are clearly correct in their insis-

---

35. Stob, "Observations," p. 251.

36. Quoted in Herman Dooyeweerd, *Roots of Western Culture: Pagan, Secular, and Christian Options,* ed. Mark Vander Vennen and Bernard Zylstra, trans. John Kraay (Toronto: Wedge Publishing Foundation, 1979), pp. 1-2.

37. Dooyeweerd, *Roots of Western Culture,* p. 3.

tence that, in an important sense, the antithesis cuts through the whole human race. We Christians certainly have no business advertising ourselves as models of righteousness. But this does not mean that we should simply set aside the notion that the antithesis functions as an oppositional relationship between two groups of identifiable people. When we downplay the reality of a deep dividing line between two actual groups of people, the believing community and the rest of humankind, we run the risk of slipping into a kind of piecemeal approach to questions of truth and goodness: the church is right about this topic, but the world is right about that one, and so on, a pattern that could weaken our sense of allegiance to a *people* called together to stand against the seductions of this present age. Or even worse, it could lead to an outlook where general standards of "reasonableness" become our sole reference point in the pursuit of righteousness.

The proper alternative is not, of course, simply to absolutize the perceptions or decisions of this or that actual Christian community. Stob and Dooyeweerd rightly caution us against such a posture. Our only true authority is the Lord who has given his Word to the church as a supremely trustworthy guide for our earthly pilgrimage. But this Lord also sends us his Spirit, who in turn distributes necessary gifts — prophecy, discernment, wisdom, knowledge — to his people in their gathered-ness. Abraham Kuyper himself regularly emphasized the centrality of this communal life for our efforts in the larger culture — to the point that *he* was actually labeled a Labadist by his national church (*Hervormed*) critics for his pleas on behalf of "a 'little flock' (Luke 12:32) in the midst of the world."[38] Kuyper insisted that "the lamp of the Christian religion only burns within [the church's] walls." And while he also argued that the light of that lamp "shines out through [the church's] windows to areas far beyond, illuminating all the sectors and associations that appear across the wide

---

38. Abraham Kuyper, "Common Grace," in James D. Bratt, ed., *Abraham Kuyper: A Centennial Reader* (Grand Rapids: Eerdmans, 1998), p. 191.

range of human life and activity,"[39] there is no question that Kuyper believed wholeheartedly that we can discern that light in the larger world only by staying very close to the lamp that burns so brightly in the midst of the gathered people of God.

Testing for Effectiveness

In 1998, the Protestant Reformed magazine *The Standard Bearer* published a series of editorials reflecting on the legacy of Abraham Kuyper, on the occasion of the centennial of Kuyper's Stone Lectures at Princeton. The editor, David Engelsma, wrote that "the worldview of common grace has proved to be a colossal failure." Since Kuyper saw his common grace views as providing the Christian community with a theological basis for exercising Christian influence on the larger culture, Engelsma observed, it is fair to examine the actual cultural fruits of a century of this theology. Certainly, he pointed out, the Netherlands and the United States are not more Reformed than they were a hundred years ago — far from it. And there are clear signs of greatly increased worldliness within the Reformed communities of both countries. In short, after a century of common grace teaching, both the world and the church have gotten worse.[40] While I would want to challenge some of the examples Engelsma offers of "thoroughly worldly" churches and schools, I do think he is right to insist that we take an honest look at the failure of common grace thought to stem the tide of wickedness so obvious in places like the Netherlands and North America. If we are to judge common grace teachings by looking for fruits of righteousness in the larger culture — surely a fair test, given the triumphalist tones in which these teachings have often been proclaimed — then we must admit to some serious shortcomings.

39. Kuyper, "Common Grace," p. 194.
40. David J. Engelsma, "The Reformed Worldview: 3. The Failure of Common Grace (cont.)," *The Standard Bearer,* September 1, 1998, p. 462.

Of course, while preserving faithfulness in the church and avoiding worldly wickedness are laudable, practical concerns, there are also other criteria that should be used in the evaluation of common grace. We must be diligent in our efforts to discover, honor, and appreciate any of God's gifts that might be at work in the larger human community, and common grace teaching has inspired many Christian people to engage in such efforts. A number of my evangelical friends, most of them not confessionally Reformed, have told me that Calvinist teachings about common grace were profoundly influential on their development as Christian intellectuals. As one accomplished evangelical scholar put it: "When I discovered the doctrine of common grace, it saved my sanity." He had long been told by the fundamentalist community that had nurtured him that all "worldly learning" was wicked. Yet he found himself responding in positive ways to elements in the writings of non-Christian thinkers. He worried that he was losing his faith until he learned about common grace and its encouragement of discerning assessment of a variety of Christian and non-Christian viewpoints. Common grace gave him a framework for pursuing his calling as a Christian scholar.

Discernment is, of course, a key requirement. We need the Spirit's guidance in our hearts and minds as we seek to identify traces of the Spirit's work in the larger creation. And we need to ground ourselves in the life and thought of that community where the Spirit is openly at work, regenerating sinners and sanctifying their inner selves. At their best, the "Labadist" voices in our midst are urging us to be clear about our primary identity. We must heed their warnings, paying careful attention to the arguments they set forth for our consideration, lest our sensitivities be dulled to the seductive power of depraved habits of thought and action.

Some of us will also be concerned, though, about other ways in which our Christian sensitivities can be dulled. Having engaged in the active assessment of that which is produced by non-Christian people, we are convinced that we have discerned on occasion that which John Calvin told us we should expect to see: an unbelieving mind that, "though fallen and perverted from its wholeness, is nevertheless clothed and ornamented with God's excellent gifts."[41] Nor do we think that Calvin was speaking too loosely when he described these gifts as flowing from "a peculiar *grace* of God."[42]

41. Calvin, *Institutes* II.2.15, p. 273.
42. Calvin, *Institutes* II.2.14, p. 273; emphasis mine.

Chapter Three

"HE SHINES IN ALL THAT'S FAIR"

In one of his published sermons, the Anglican theologian Austin Farrer describes his efforts to reconcile his theological convictions about sin and unbelief with his daily encounters with flesh-and-blood unbelievers. In his days at Oxford University, he would often attend one of the campus evangelistic services that were regularly held for the university community. There the preacher would typically set forth a stark contrast between belief and unbelief. We must submit without reserve to the claims of the gospel, the evangelist would urge; no compromises with worldliness are permitted. Such preaching had a powerful influence on Farrer's way of viewing reality. It allowed him to "see how blessed it would be if we could live for God alone. Compared to the clearness of such a life, our present confused muddle of aims, our self-indulgence, our meanness, and our vanity [would] seem dark indeed."

But then on his way home after the service he would run into a non-Christian friend who would urge Farrer to join him for a drink at a pub. Farrer knew that to accept the person's invitation would signal a weakening of his spiritual resolve. But his friend would persist, and reluctantly Farrer would agree to join him. And sure enough, Farrer would soon find himself thoroughly enjoying these relaxed moments. The friend's humor was admittedly irreverent, but Farrer would actually find such humor to be "all the better for being a bit wicked." Not that this person was an out-and-out atheist, but he clearly fell into the evangelist's category of the unconverted. As the evening wore on, the starkly drawn lines of the evangelist's portrayal began to blur in Farrer's mind. They did not seem to comport well with the pleasure of this friend's company — so much so that Farrer was tempted to say to himself, "How absurd! Old Robin Johnson a citizen in the kingdom of darkness! The whole thing's nonsense! Have another drink."[1]

Farrer knows, of course, that a Christian cannot simply leave it at that, so he struggles to make theological sense of this kind of experience. How Farrer himself deals with the tension theologically is not quite enough to satisfy my Calvinist soul: he decides that he can simply pray for his friend's conversion even as he celebrates the goodness of the sinner's "mere humanity." That may be roughly the right place to end up, but his way of resolving the struggle seems a bit quick to me. Nevertheless, the tension that he describes is indeed a real one. The old saw about desiring heaven for the climate and hell for the company may overstate the case — and it may also slip over the edge into blasphemy. But it does point to a set of issues that have to be addressed if some of us are to maintain our theological and spiritual sanity.

Extra-Salvific Assessments

Here, then, is the question that I want now to explore. How do we take with utmost seriousness the need to be clear about the lines between belief and unbelief, between those who live within the boundaries of saving grace and those who do not, while at the same time

1. Austin Farrer, "The Charms of Unbelief," in *A Faith of Our Own* (Cleveland: The World Publishing Co., 1960), pp. 13-14.

maintaining an openness to — even an active appreciation for — all that is good and beautiful and true that takes place outside of those boundaries?

No Christian attempt to answer this question can fail to attend to the closely related topic of *God's* dispositions in this regard. This is certainly Calvinism's entree into the discussion. Our likes and dislikes must be brought into conformity to God's approvals and disapprovals. And when we restrict our focus to salvific matters, the basic patterns of God's likes and dislikes are very clear. God is surely favorably disposed toward the elect, having graciously chosen to point them in the direction of a glorious heavenly destiny. And he is not favorably disposed toward the non-elect, since he has, in the words of the Canons of Dort, "decreed to leave [them] in the common misery into which they have willfully plunged themselves."[2]

A crucial question to ask, however, is whether salvific categories are adequate to cover all of God's dispositions toward human beings, both redeemed and unredeemed. More specifically, is the ultimate destiny of human beings the only thing that God thinks about in assessing what we think, feel, and do? Does he care about the actions and achievements of non-elect persons in a way that is not linked directly to issues of individual salvation? These questions are at the heart of the idea of common grace.

Let me substitute for Austin Farrer's story one that has more direct relevance for Calvinists. In his biography of George Whitefield, Harry Stout reports that during his extensive time in North America, the Calvinist evangelist formed a deep friendship with Benjamin Franklin. Anyone who knows anything about the convictions of these two men has to be a bit surprised by the fact of this friendship. Whitefield exhibited all of the characteristics that are usually associated with the term "Puritan": a strong affirmation of Calvinist doc-

---

2. Canons of Dort, Head I, Art. 15, in Philip Schaff, ed., *The Creeds of Christendom, with a History and Critical Notes,* vol. III (Grand Rapids: Baker Books, 1996), p. 584.

trines, a devotion to moral rectitude, and a stern demeanor. Franklin on the other hand was well known as a religious skeptic given to irreverent comments; he also had the reputation for being a womanizer.[3] Although we obviously do not know enough simply to label Franklin as one of the non-elect, from the available evidence he certainly gave every indication of placing himself in that category. Nor is there is any reason to think that Whitefield had a different assessment of the state of Franklin's eternal soul. We have to assume, then, that the main reason why the Calvinist evangelist chose to spend time with the religious skeptic was that he simply enjoyed his company.

Now here is what I consider an important question: Did God approve of the fact that Whitefield enjoyed spending time with Benjamin Franklin? In one sense, of course, any Calvinist might allow an affirmative answer to that question: there may have been some important God-ordained goal for which the friendship between the two was an important predestined means. But I want to focus the question on the friendship in itself. Did God approve of the ways in which Whitefield enjoyed his relationship with Franklin? Did the Lord see the friendly give-and-take between the two of them as a pleasant thing to behold? Was God gratified by the ways in which their written correspondence was crafted? Was Whitefield's *commitment* to Franklin — his caring about his friend's physical well-being, his desire to stay in Franklin's home when he visited Philadelphia, his pain over some of Franklin's specific misdeeds — was all of that something God *wanted* to happen, simply because God himself cares about what goes on in a friendship, even when one of the friends is not numbered among the elect? Again, how do we take with utmost seriousness the need to be clear about the lines between belief and unbelief, between those who live within the boundaries of saving grace and those who do not, while at the same time maintaining an openness to and active appreciation for all that is good and

3. Cf. Harry S. Stout, *The Divine Dramatist: George Whitefield and the Rise of Modern Evangelicalism* (Grand Rapids, Mich.: Eerdmans, 1991), pp. 220-33.

beautiful and true that takes place outside of those boundaries? And in beginning to explore that question, I have already linked it to an even more basic question: In our appreciation, as elect people, of the good and the beautiful and the true that takes place outside of those boundaries, are we in some important sense imitating *God's* appreciation of such things?

In the event that some Calvinist wants to avoid this question by insisting that there really is nothing outside the boundaries of special grace that God can be rightly thought of as seeing as "good and beautiful and true," then I must hasten to point out that there are obvious counterexamples to this denial in God's dealing with the *non*-human creation. For example, in the creation account of Genesis 1, God created swarms of living things to swim in the waters, and when he was finished he looked at this swarming and expressed satisfaction in what he saw. It takes no great stretch of the imagination to think that God actually took *pleasure* in seeing the eagle take flight for the first time, for the psalmist tells us that the Lord rejoices in what he has made (Ps. 104:31). There is good reason to believe that the Lord is gratified by glowing sunsets and ocean waves breaking on a rocky coastline and a cherry tree in bloom and the speed of a leopard on the chase — and all of this without any necessary reference to elect and non-elect human beings.

A Larger Glorying

I don't think I am stretching Calvinist patterns of thought very much in making this case. If God is *glorified* by his non-human creation — which seems to be a fairly modest claim to endorse — then it seems reasonable to assume that God *takes delight* in those non-human created phenomena. And then it also seems to be quite plausible to assume that God takes delight in various *human* states of affairs, even when they are displayed in the lives of non-elect human beings.

35

This is where I find Herman Hoeksema's thought — and the formulations of many other supralapsarians discussing God's creating purposes — most puzzling. Here is a typical Hoeksema comment: "in the counsel of God all other things in heaven and on earth are designed as means to the realization of both election and reprobation, and therefore, of the glory of Christ and His church."[4] Here is another: "All the things of the present life are but means to an eternal end."[5] So the goal of bringing the elect and the reprobate to their eternal destinies, for Hoeksema, is *the* divine goal, and all other seemingly independent goals are really to be viewed as means to the attainment of that one goal. Thus Hoeksema is committed to a perspective in which the paths of the eagle's flight and the ocean's waves are ordained by God simply as means to the goal of bringing human beings to their foreordained destinies, and in which the divine delight in such things is necessarily connected to the role they play in fulfilling the eternal salvific decree.

I find this belief no less puzzling when I extend it — as surely it must be extended from Hoeksema's perspective — to the actions of non-elect human beings. Let me be concrete: I think God takes delight in Benjamin Franklin's wit and in Tiger Woods's putts and in some well-crafted narrative paragraphs in a Salman Rushdie novel, even if these accomplishments are in fact achieved by non-Christian people. And I am convinced that God's delight in these phenomena does not come because they bring the elect to glory and the non-elect to eternal separation from the divine presence. I think God enjoys these things for their *own* sakes.

---

4. Herman Hoeksema, *Reformed Dogmatics* (Grand Rapids: Reformed Free Publishing Association, 1966), p. 165.

5. Herman Hoeksema, *The Protestant Reformed Churches in America: Their Origin, Early History and Doctrine* (Grand Rapids: First Protestant Reformed Church, 1936), p. 314.

Moral Approval

The examples that I have given thus far can be subsumed, broadly speaking, under the category of the *aesthetic*. The above examples of God's delight do not necessarily involve moral approval of the "inner" lives of non-elect people. When an unbelieving poet makes use of an apt metaphor, or when a foul-mouthed major league outfielder leaps high into the air to make a stunning catch, we can think of God as enjoying the event without necessarily approving of anything in the *agents* involved — just as *we* might give high marks to a rhetorical flourish by a politician whose views on public policy we despise. But I want now to push the argument a step further: I think that God also gives positive *moral* appraisals to non-elect persons.

During the radical political protests of the 1960s, it was common to distinguish between those who had a vested interest in protecting "the system" and those who were willing to take a stand against the political-economic status quo. The writer Norman Mailer provocatively characterized these two groups as "sheriffs" and "outlaws" — with the latter group holding the sorts of moral and political views of which Mailer approved. When many of Mailer's friends greeted John F. Kennedy's election to the presidency with considerable enthusiasm, Mailer was convinced that they were deluded. Don't be deceived, he warned them; for all of Kennedy's personal charm and his glowing talk about "new frontiers," he was still a sheriff who was out to frustrate the cause of the outlaws. But I remember reading somewhere Mailer's account of how he reacted to President Kennedy's death: in the weeks after the president was assassinated, Mailer reported that he was surprised to find himself slipping into a deep depression. Obviously, in spite of the role he had assigned to Kennedy in his classificatory scheme, he had somehow formed a strong admiration for the young president. But how could this be? Why would he feel such a sense of loss over the death of a powerful sheriff? Mailer solved his puzzle by the creation of a new category: Kennedy had indeed been a sheriff, but Mailer decided Kennedy had been "an outlaw's sheriff."

I must confess that I also find it necessary to create third categories on a regular basis. As a Calvinist, I accept the fundamental classification of humankind into two categories, the elect and the non-elect, and I believe that while we are all totally depraved, God enables his redeemed people to perform acts of righteousness that would not be possible apart from divine grace. But I also witness — regularly, I must emphasize — acts of kindness on the part of the unredeemed that clearly seem to be in conformity to revealed standards of righteousness. Nor am I inclined simply to dismiss these acts as nothing more than well-disguised deeds of unrighteousness. There is, for example, a large moral difference between the acts of the courageous, unbelieving white people who risked and even lost their lives in the American civil rights struggle of the 1960s and the acts of those unbelievers who willfully carried out Hitler's orders in exterminating the Jews.

The recognition of a need for creating a third category is not absent from the Reformed confessions. While the Heidelberg Catechism makes the unqualified judgment that apart from the regenerating grace of God we are incapable of "*any* good,"[6] the Canons of Dort introduce an appropriate nuance, telling us that we are all "by nature children of wrath, incapable of any *saving* good"[7] — thus leaving open the possibility of deeds that are morally laudable without meriting salvation.

A third category is also suggested, albeit in a guarded manner, in the Westminster Confession's treatment of moral goodness:

Works done by unregenerate men, although for the matter of them they may be things which God commands, and of good use both to

6. Heidelberg Catechism, Question and Answer 8, in Schaff, *Creeds,* Vol. III, p. 310; emphasis mine.

7. Canons of Dort, Heads III and IV, art. 3, in Schaff, *Creeds,* Vol. III, p. 588; emphasis mine.

themselves and others, yet because they proceed not from a heart purified by faith, nor are done in a right manner, according to the Word, nor to a right end, the glory of God; they are therefore sinful, and cannot please God, or make a man meet to receive grace from God. And yet their neglect of them is more sinful and displeasing to God.[8]

In spite of the decidedly negative tone of these comments, the Westminster divines are actually making room for a measure of divine approval regarding deeds performed by the unregenerate that nonetheless conform to God's revealed standards. Since the *"neglect* of [such deeds] is *more* sinful and displeasing to God," such good works at least are *less displeasing* to God. The implication here is that there is a category of moral acts performed by the unregenerate that are *more pleasing* to God than their *non*-performance would be.

Divine Empathy

But now I want to move into even larger territory. Both defenders and opponents of the idea of common grace have regularly described it as involving an attitude of divine favor, albeit not necessarily a saving favor, toward elect and non-elect alike. I want now to frame the issues in terms of divine *empathy*. Is it plausible for us to think that there are times when God looks favorably upon the non-elect in this sense: that he has empathy for their very real experiences of joy and sadness, just as he certainly does for those of the elect?

This question for me has direct connections to some very practical interests that I have in trying to understand theologically what I think of as *common grace ministries*. For example, a Calvinist involved in ministering to people in a hospital-sponsored alcoholism recovery program once described his situation to me very poignantly: "I regularly

8. Westminster Confession of Faith, Chapter XVI, Article 7, in Schaff, *Creeds,* Vol. III, p. 636.

see people move from a rather desperate kind of bondage to new dimensions of freedom in their lives. The change is often very dramatic. Yet it isn't at all obvious that in experiencing this release from addiction they have been regenerated in the classic sense. Their lives have been transformed, but they have not come to know Jesus. I do want them to become Christians. Yet I also want to celebrate what looks for all the world to me like a 'grace' occurrence in their lives. My Reformed theology seems to lack the appropriate categories for all of this."

He is right. Certainly our typical formulations of a theology of common grace do not apply directly to his situation. The 1924 Christian Reformed declarations, as discussed earlier, addressed these three areas: (1) "natural" blessings, such as rain and sunshine; (2) the restraining of evil in human affairs; and (3) positive acts of civic righteousness. These three categories have little to do with the seeming occurrences of grace that many of us see in the lives of non-Christians.

Take the case of a Christian therapist counseling a non-Christian couple whose marriage has been seriously wounded by the husband's adulterous affair. The therapist helps them to be honest about the hurts and fears and angers that have surrounded the infidelity. Finally, a moment comes when the husband tearfully acknowledges the pain he has caused and asks his wife to forgive him. She reaches out with a newfound tenderness toward him. They embrace, both of them sobbing. It is clear that they intend to build a new life together. They have not been "saved" in the process, but the therapist is convinced that she has witnessed — and has been privileged to be a human instrument in — a powerful display of healing grace. She senses that she has reinforced the kinds of behaviors and attitudes that God wants for human beings.

Once again, this therapy does not fall within the summary account of the workings of common grace as set forth in the Christian Reformed Church's 1924 declarations. It certainly doesn't fall under the category of "natural" blessings, along with sunshine and rain. Nor does the therapist want to see it merely as a case of the *restraint*

"He Shines in All That's Fair"

of sin. In common grace discussions, the restraining of sin has often been illustrated by the example of a rabid dog that is kept from doing all the harm it might otherwise do by being pulled back on a leash. That kind of image will not satisfy the Christian therapist's strong sense that something positively healing has occurred in the lives of the married couple. Her story can be better illustrated by that of a dog that suddenly starts wagging its tail and licking the hand of the person it growled at only a few minutes before. The third category in the Christian Reformed list, the one that posits positive acts of civic righteousness, comes closest to describing her encounter. But the plausibility of the cases usually associated with this category is strengthened in Calvinist thought by their role in the larger providential scheme of things: they make it easier for the church to do its task, or they promote the maintenance and preservation of the civic order. Calvinists have focused on civic issues in talking about common grace because historically Calvinist thinkers have been especially interested in the promotion of societal order. But I do not think that those interests serve to illuminate what is going on in this therapeutic example. The issue here is not primarily the preservation of order, nor how this particular transaction between a non-believing husband and wife will contribute to the well-being of the Christian community. This case looks like a very good thing in itself, and a situation where Christian people can surmise, with some degree of confidence, that God is pleased by what has happened.

I am intentionally focusing here on specific cases seldom looked at in discussions of common grace. What would a theologian who denies common grace say of the case I just posed? Was the Christian therapist simply carried away by misleading emotions when she shed tears of happiness over these gestures of reconciliation? Was she wrong in thinking her tears were *godly* tears? Was she theologically confused in her strong sense that the Lord himself was involved in the joy of this reconciliation?

But a Calvinist theology of empathy must also look carefully at less pleasant emotions. For the sake of clarity in some important matters regarding this more negative empathy, I want to look at a case of what I consider to be unspeakable cruelty. It is not the kind of example that lends itself to dispassionate analysis, but it is important, for the purpose of this discussion, to look honestly at an extreme case of negative empathy. During an "ethnic cleansing" rampage in Eastern Europe, some soldiers raped a Muslim woman. Just as they were finishing their wicked business, her baby began to cry. She pleaded with them not to kill her, but to leave her alone so that she might nurse her child. One of the soldiers responded by grabbing her baby, cutting its head off, and placing it on her breast.

A horrible story to tell. But it is precisely our sense of horror, of outrage, that we must look at and attempt to understand theologically. Let us assume that this woman was not one of God's elect. I must confess that this assumption has absolutely no bearing on my own overwhelming sense of anger and sorrow every time I think about this terrible episode. Nor can I imagine any Calvinist, whatever his or her particular theology of common grace, not having the same kind of reaction. Certainly our hearts instinctively go out to the woman. Is this a sanctified instinct? Is it something we will come to think and feel differently about as Calvinists once we have thought it through theologically? On an even more basic level: Does the heart of God also break when something like this happens? Is the eternal destiny of the people involved the only thing that influences God's assessment when he views such an incident? If that *is* his only basis for assessing his relationship to the situation, then why do we feel such empathy for the woman? Why our own deep sense of violation on her behalf over the human cruelty that has been inflicted on her and her child?

The Need for an Explanation

One of the few Calvinist writers on common grace who does address the more intimate empathy-invoking cases I consider here is Abraham Kuyper. He acknowledges the need to account for these kinds of situations when he distinguishes between what he labels the "interior" and "exterior" operations of common grace. The latter label covers collective sorts of achievements, such as advances in scientific knowledge and the flourishing of the arts. The former, however, "is operative," says Kuyper, "wherever civic virtue, a sense of domesticity, natural love, the practice of human virtue, the improvement of the public conscience, integrity, mutual loyalty among people, and a feeling for piety leaven life."[9]

The examples that Kuyper lists require theological explanation, and those Calvinist thinkers who reject any sort of "interior" working of grace in the lives of the non-elect would seem to have the more challenging explanatory task. It certainly seems obvious — to me at least — that the more natural way to view these cases is to think that God judges the inner states of the unbelieving couple who have experienced marital reconciliation to be better than the inner states associated with their former alienation, and that the Muslim mother's love of her child is better than the attitude of a parent who is not concerned for her child's well-being. To insist that all of the subjective experiences of the non-elect are of equal value in the sight of God requires some fairly arbitrary explanations — much like the arguments of those who insist all human acts are completely selfish in motivation, so that throwing oneself on a live grenade to save the lives of comrades is selfish in the same sense and to the same degree as robbing a bank and killing everyone who witnesses the crime.

Kuyper's insistence that there is a gracious divine operation that works in the "interior" lives of the non-elect provides us with a plausible Calvinist interpretation on at least two levels. First, it provides a rationale for what seems to be a strong Christian disposition not only to give a positive assessment to many "external" actions of non-Christian people but also to attribute laudable "internal" motives

---

9. Abraham Kuyper, "Common Grace," in James D. Bratt, ed., *Abraham Kuyper: A Centennial Reader* (Grand Rapids: Eerdmans, 1998), p. 181.

for those actions. In this view, the non-Christian husband who asked his wife for forgiveness could very well have possessed a morally appropriate motive for doing so — for example, he could have been genuinely sorry for violating the trust that is necessary for sustaining a marital relationship.

But second, Kuyper recognizes that when we sinners do in fact operate with laudable motives for doing the right thing, we cannot do so by our unaided moral powers, but only by virtue of a divine operation at work within us. In the redeemed person this is clearly possible because of the regenerating and sanctifying power of the Holy Spirit. In his lengthy discussion of the doctrine of the Holy Spirit, Kuyper notes that only the Third Person of the Trinity can effect "the formation of character, and the disposition of the whole person" in the life of the believer.[10] If unredeemed persons, then, also exhibit the "internal" motives that we recognize as the work of the Spirit in the lives of the elect, here too the Holy Spirit must be at work, since "the work of the Holy Spirit consists in leading all creation *to its destiny*, the final purpose of which is the glory of God," and this "glory in creation appears in various degrees and ways."[11] This larger work of the Holy Spirit supplements the salvific designs of God in the world by working "independently to bring about in all its dimensions and in defiance of Satanic opposition and human sin the full emergence of what God had in mind when he planted those nuclei of higher development in our race."[12]

John Bolt nicely summarizes this admittedly mysterious aspect of the Spirit's work in the form of a series of probing questions:

> If we can theologically conceive of the Holy Spirit giving the gift of life to an unbeliever and even further giving an unbeliever natural gifts (intelligence, musical ability, healthy and athletic body), why

10. Abraham Kuyper, *The Work of the Holy Spirit*, trans. Henri de Vries (New York: Funk and Wagnalls, 1900), p. 24.

11. Kuyper, *Work of the Holy Spirit*, p. 22.

12. Kuyper, "Common Grace," p. 179.

could we not conceive of a work of God the Holy Spirit that *providentially* influences an unbeliever's heart and will so that he or she does constructive and externally virtuous acts rather than destructive ones? What is the theological problem, for example, with suggesting that the Lord's anointed servant Cyrus's decree returning the Jews to their homeland was providentially influenced by the Spirit of God? What is the problem, particularly if we continue to insist that such deeds are not at all "good" in the Catechism's sense but that the work of God's Spirit is simply a means by which our Lord governs human history and thus influences people to do acts of which he approves because "they have reference to an end of which he [not only] approves" but has in fact decreed?[13]

"Grace Is Everywhere"

In the powerful ending to *The Diary of a Country Priest,* a novel by Georges Bernanos, the priest whose life and ministry is chronicled throughout the book lies dying, and the fellow priest who has been called to administer the last rites has not yet arrived. His friend expresses regret, but as the priest dies he utters these words: "Does it matter? Grace is everywhere."[14]

Some Calvinists have given their own meaning to this "grace is everywhere" motif. Abraham Kuyper, for example, saw grace not only as operating broadly in *human* affairs; he argued that it also abounds in *nature in general.* The very continuation of the creation as such, Kuyper insisted, is due to the sustaining power of God. Without his direct upholding activity, creation would self-destruct.

Not all adherents to the common grace idea agree with Kuyper

13. John Bolt, "Common Grace, Theonomy, and Civic Good: The Temptations of Calvinist Politics," *Calvin Theological Journal* 33, no. 2 (November 2000): 237.

14. Georges Bernanos, *Diary of a Country Priest* (New York: Carroll and Graf Publishers, 1989), p. 298.

on this point. Henry Van Til, for one, complains that "Kuyper resorts to theological speculation when he maintains that except for common grace the world would have fallen apart, as a vase breaks into shivers when one removes its support."[15] Van Til is right, of course, in discerning an element of theological speculation here. But it is difficult to defend his further observation that Kuyper's view on this topic "is not in the best tradition of Calvinist thought."[16]

Given the strong emphasis that Calvinists have placed on the sovereign freedom of God, it should not surprise us that they have often carried this theme directly over into their depictions of God's relationship to the created order. In his remarkably lucid essay on "Miracles," for example, Henry Stob argues that in God's dealings with the natural order, God "is bound by no external rules and he is accountable to no one but himself. He traces his own paths through all that he has made." Thus, says Stob, our human formulations of what we call "'the laws of nature' . . . are nothing but our transcripts of God's 'customary ways.' They are not prior to, but after God; they record his habits. They 'hold' because God is wont to travel the same way; but they do not bind him."[17]

John Calvin himself gave considerable attention to this notion that the created order is held together at each moment by the sovereign decree of God. In her masterful study of Calvin's understanding of God's relationship to the created order, Susan Schreiner points to the centrality of this theme:

> The joy that Calvin took in the wonders of nature has been well documented by Calvin scholars, but it is necessary to remember that this joy presupposed the inherent fragility of creation; nature does not, in Calvin's view, remain ordered in and of itself. To Calvin, the

---

15. Henry R. Van Til, *The Calvinistic Concept of Culture* (Grand Rapids: Baker Book House, 1959), p. 230.

16. Van Til, *Calvinistic Concept of Culture*, p. 231.

17. Henry Stob, *Theological Reflections: Essays on Related Themes* (Grand Rapids: Eerdmans, 1981), p. 24.

inherent character of creation was not conducive to order; only a great divine power could preserve the grand orderliness that we perceive in the universe. The stability of nature depends on "the continual rejoicing of God in his works."[18]

For Calvin, as Schreiner notes, the world is engulfed at every moment "by a 'flood of iniquity' which must be continually restrained by God lest it rush forth and engulf the earth."[19] The iniquitous threat here is not primarily a human one. Without God's constant "bridling" activity all of creation would slip into disarray. And not only must God keep the chaotic waters within their appointed bounds, he must also continually "bridle the animals lest they come forth and devour people and he must bridle people lest they devour each other. For Calvin, the 'bridle of divine providence' curbs the wicked and the devil lest they completely overturn all order and make life unlivable."[20]

Some commentators have suggested that Calvin's worries about the fragility of the created order stemmed from a very personal fear of chaos.[21] If so, it could still be argued that the Reformer's neuroses have resulted in some fairly healthy theology. The notion that the world as we know it is in a very fundamental way on the brink of chaos may not have played well in recent centuries, when so many thinkers took it as a given that reality exhibited an intrinsic rational ordering. But in our own time, when the very idea of *cosmos* has been "deconstructed," with the result that order is often viewed as a hu-

---

18. Susan E. Schreiner, *The Theater of His Glory: Nature and the Natural Order in the Thought of John Calvin* (Grand Rapids: Baker Book House, 1991), p. 28. In her account of Calvin's views on this subject, Schreiner cites materials from a variety of his sermons and commentaries, especially those on Job and the Psalms.

19. Schreiner, *Theater of His Glory,* p. 29.

20. Schreiner, *Theater of His Glory,* p. 30.

21. See William J. Bouwsma, *John Calvin: A Sixteenth Century Portrait* (New York: Oxford University Press, 1988), especially his chapter "Calvin's Anxiety," pp. 32-48.

man creation rather than a reality to be discovered, we would do well to consider anew the explanatory benefits of a theological perspective that celebrates the power of a sovereign God who alone can protect us from the very real threat of chaos. The tenor of our times makes proclaiming a Calvinist version of the "grace is everywhere" theme especially important.

The "Grace" Question

As he reaches the conclusion of his own rather cautiously formulated case in favor of a theology of common grace, Henry Van Til raises the important question of whether common grace is indeed "grace" in any straightforward sense of the word. He decides that it is best "to place the term 'common grace' in quotation marks," because it seems a little odd to equate what he considers to be the very real "beneficent goodness of God to the non-elect sinners" with the redemptive "blessings which God bestows upon elect sinners in and through Jesus Christ, the Mediator."[22]

Van Til is right to raise this caution. At the heart of all evangelical religion is the sense of wonder at God's saving purposes that is captured so movingly in Charles Wesley's eloquently expressed questions:

> And can it be that I should gain
> An int'rest in the Saviour's blood?
> Died He for me who caused His pain?
> For me who Him to death pursued?
> Amazing love! How can it be
> That Thou my God shouldst die for me?

When our theology of grace focuses in a central way on the marvelous display of unmerited favor that occurred at Calvary, when we fix

22. Van Til, *Calvinistic Concept of Culture*, p. 244.

our sights on the wondrously incomprehensible event of, in Spurgeon's words, "the just Ruler dying for the unjust rebel,"[23] do we really want also to use the term "grace" to describe the power that holds molecules together, that superintends the cycles of the seasons, that plants in unredeemed hearts the capacity for composing pleasant melodies, and that fosters in unredeemed people a disposition to live peaceably with their neighbors?

I do not think we should take this question lightly. Those of us fond of employing Bonhoeffer's notion of "cheap grace" to criticize beneficiaries of God's mercy who refuse to promote the cause of justice in the world need also to think about the ways we cheapen grace when we claim its presence in acts of mere justice unaccompanied by pleas of mercy before the throne of the One who alone issues decrees that are perfectly true and just. We do well, then, to heed Van Til's misgivings about any talk of common grace that does not put at least mental quotation marks around the word "grace."

Still, it is true that in disputes about the reality of common grace, both defenders and critics have identified the idea of a non-saving attitude of divine favor as the central issue. In this sense it is meaningful to describe, for example, the very act of creating the world as a work of grace. God did not have to create anything. All that exists owes its reality to the fact that God looks favorably upon its existence. And it also makes good sense to think of God as showing active benevolence to his non-elect human creatures. There is a divine empathy that is evoked when a non-Christian woman is brutally raped, or when marital reconciliation takes place between two thoroughgoing secularists. God also takes a positive interest in how unbelievers use God-given talents to produce works of beauty and goodness. For lack of a better term, the power that is at work in these situations deserves to be thought of as a kind of "grace."

23. Charles Spurgeon, *All of Grace*, http://www.spurgeon.org/all_of_g.htm, section 5.

Multiple Divine Purposes

The underlying view I am endorsing here posits multiple divine purposes in the world. To state it plainly: I am insisting that as God unfolds his plan for his creation, he is interested in more than one thing. Alongside of God's clear concern about the eternal destiny of individuals are his designs for the larger creation. Herman Bavinck and Abraham Kuyper were both clear on this point: they were convinced that the Bible explicitly encourages us to expect an eschatological ingathering of the fruits of humankind's cultural labors. A key text for their argument was Revelation 21:24-26, where the apostle foresees that the nations of the earth will walk by the light of the Holy City, "and the kings of the earth will bring their glory into it.... People will bring into it the glory and the honor of the nations."

To be sure, the Spirit-guided author is pointing here to something that is enshrouded in mystery. How will the state of things in our present world contribute to this final manifestation of glory? And how is it possible that the honor and glory of pagan cultures can be brought into a City where "nothing unclean will enter in" (Rev. 21:27)? And to what degree can we use and enjoy in the here and now those things from which the curse has not yet been removed?

Those of us who endorse the idea of common grace would do well to recognize the ways in which its teachings frequently have fostered a triumphalist spirit that has encouraged false hopes for a premature transformation of sinful culture. But for all of that, the theologians of common grace have nonetheless been right to insist that the God who is unfolding his multiple purposes in this present age also calls his people to be agents of those diverse Kingdom goals. It is important for us in these difficult days to cultivate an appropriate Calvinist sense of modesty and humility in our efforts at cultural faithfulness. But we cannot give up on the important task — which the theologians of common grace have correctly urged upon us — of actively working to discern God's complex designs in the midst of our deeply wounded world.

This issue of multiple divine purposes is obviously a point of contention among Calvinists. Indeed, I am convinced that it is the underlying issue at stake in the longstanding intra-Calvinist debates between "infralapsarians" and "supralapsarians." While those arguments have often been depicted as a prime example of how theological discussion can get sidetracked into useless disputations, I think that assessment is misguided; the infralapsarian-supralapsarian discussions actually address fundamental questions about God's purposes in the world. In the next chapter I will explore the relevance of those debates for our understanding of the ways in which the Creator's glory "shines in all that's fair."

Chapter Four

"INFRA-" VERSUS "SUPRA-"

In 1973, Theodore Kreps returned to Calvin College to receive a Distinguished Alumnus Award. Kreps had finished his studies at Calvin in 1917, earned a Harvard doctorate in economics, and gone on to gain an international reputation as a business economist, spending the last three decades of his academic career at Stanford University. At a reception held in his honor, Professor Kreps told me how he had made his way to Grand Rapids, Michigan, a half century earlier, to begin his undergraduate education. Raised in the small Dutch Calvinist farming community of Prinsburg, Minnesota, he had little hope of getting a college education until he heard that the Christian Reformed congregations of Pella, Iowa, were sponsoring an essay contest, the first prize being a tuition scholarship to Calvin College. He hopped a freight train to Iowa, and when he arrived he discovered that he had twenty-four hours to produce an essay on the assigned topic, "The Debate between the Infra- and the Supra-lapsarians." He composed the prize-winning entry while sitting on a park bench. When he finished telling me the story, I asked him which side of the debate he defended in his essay. "Oh," he replied without a moment's pause, "I've always been an 'infra,' of course!"

I was intrigued by the "of course" part of his unhesitating answer. Not that I would have expected him to endorse supralapsarianism. The infralapsarian view has always been the majority opinion in the Calvinist tradition, with supralapsarianism tolerated at best. What impressed me about Professor Kreps's response was that he had a position at all on the subject. The tendency these days, at least among mainline Reformed thinkers, is to see the infralapsarian versus supralapsarian debate as a pseudo-puzzle. But Kreps was obviously a thoughtful person, and I sensed a seriousness in his report concerning his infralapsarian sympathies. His comments inspired me to make a note to myself to do some exploring someday in this theological neighborhood. This essay is a modest step in that direction.

The Traditional Formulations

The two positions as traditionally formulated propose two different sequences for God's decisions to create the world, permit the fall of humankind, and elect some persons to eternal salvation while assigning others to reprobation. The supralapsarian insists that God first decreed that there would be a certain group of elect human beings and another group of reprobates; only then did God decide to make all of this happen by creating the world and permitting the fall into sin. Thus the decree of election and reprobation was prior to, or "supra," the decision to permit the fall. Infralapsarians propose a different sequence: first God decided to create the world; then God decided to permit the fall; only after these decrees did the divine decision occur with regard to election and reprobation. Thus God's electing and reprobating purposes were subordinate to, or "infra," the decision to create a world that would come to be plagued by sin.

Among Reformed confessional documents, the canons produced by the 1618-19 Synod of Dordrecht provide the most detailed treatment of these matters. It is generally agreed that the major thrust of these canons is along infralapsarian lines, describing God as choosing to elect individuals from out of a larger human race already fallen:

Election is the unchangeable purpose of God, whereby, before the foundation of the world, he hath, out of mere grace, according to the sovereign good pleasure of his own will, chosen, from the whole human race, which had fallen through their own fault, from their primitive state of rectitude, into sin and destruction, a certain number of persons to redemption in Christ, whom he from eternity appointed the Mediator and head of the elect, and the foundation of salvation.[1]

But while the Dordrecht synod obviously favored the infralapsarian scheme, it did not condemn the supralapsarian alternative. The official pronouncements of Calvinist churches have typically expressed a similar willingness to tolerate both positions, as exemplified in the "Conclusions of Utrecht" issued in 1905 by the Reformed *(Gereformeerde)* Churches of the Netherlands. While the delegates to that Dutch synod reaffirmed the infralapsarian view as the official teaching of their churches, they also judged that since "the Synod of Dort has made no pronouncement on this disputed point," it is important for Reformed Christians not to "molest anyone who personally holds the supralapsarian view."[2]

Typical Objections

Again, however, there are many theologians who see both of these formulations as fundamentally misguided. They see many similarities between the infra- versus supra- debate and the "angels on the head of a pin" discussion in medieval scholasticism. For many

1. *The Canons of the Synod of Dort,* Head I, art. 7, in Philip Schaff, ed., *The Creeds of Christendom, with a History and Critical Notes,* Vol. III (Grand Rapids: Baker Books, 1996), p. 582.
2. "Conclusies van Utrecht, 1905," English translation, in Christian Reformed Church's *Acts of Synod, 1942* (Grand Rapids: Christian Reformed Publishing House, 1942), p. 352.

within the Reformed tradition, it is an embarrassing example of how their own patterns of theologizing can run amok; for external critics of the tradition, it provides the basis for a *reductio ad absurdum* of the system's basic premises.

More specifically, objections to the debate seem to fall into at least three categories. The first sees this kind of discussion as exhibiting an intellectual arrogance. One of the sons of the great British political leader William Wilberforce told a story in his diary about his father's reading of a well-known Calvinist writer. The elder Wilberforce, obviously exasperated with what he found on the printed page, exclaimed, "Oh how unlike is this to the Scripture! He writes as if he had sat at the Council Board with the Almighty!"[3] Wilberforce was expressing a common complaint about Calvinism, one echoed by Alfred Kazin in the opening line of his recent study of the role of religion in American literature: "In the beginning at New England our writers were Calvinists, absolutely sure of God and all His purposes."[4]

While this complaint — that Calvinists think they can discern patterns of divine thought and action that should be left to the realm of mystery — may have some legitimacy, we ought not to endorse it too quickly. Whether Calvinists have been wrong in sketching out infralapsarian and supralapsarian scenarios cannot be determined simply by pointing out the speculative nature of their theories. The theological task as such thrives on speculation. Given that fact, we should at least be willing to test out Karl Barth's insistence that these doctrinal formulations do have a kind of "ecclesiatical utility,"[5] as well as Richard Muller's more specific claim that while Calvinism's fondness for constructing systems about

3. David Newsome, *The Parting of Friends: The Wilberforces and Henry Manning* (Grand Rapids: Eerdmans, 1993), pp. 47-48.

4. Alfred Kazin, *God and the American Writer* (New York: Alfred A. Knopf, 1997), p. 3.

5. Karl Barth, *Church Dogmatics*, vol. II/2, ed. G. W. Bromiley and T. F. Torrance (Edinburgh: T & T Clark, 1957), p. 131.

God's eternal purposes "is indeed a form of theological speculation, . . . it is a speculation guided by the needs of piety."[6]

A second kind of objection is closely related to the first: some believe that infralapsarians and supralapsarians wrongly assume the issues they are addressing are susceptible to logical argumentation. Put simply, their objection is that the infra- versus supra- debate is a clear example of logical thinking gone wild. Here too we should not endorse this objection quickly. Indeed, it isn't even clear that the defender of the infra- versus supra- debate needs to accept the terms of this objection. Instead of seeing the situation simply in terms of the use of logic, why not think of infralapsarianism and supralapsarianism as exercises in narrative theology? In this way of construing the discussion, the proponents of these two perspectives are setting forth alternative narratives that are meant to make sense of matters that would otherwise remain disconnected. Herman Hoeksema rightly warns us against seeing infralapsarianism and supralapsarianism as informing us about "what is first or last in the decree of God." Rather, he tells us, they attempt to answer such questions as: "what in those decrees is conceived as purpose, and what as means? What is the main object in those decrees, and what is subordinate and subservient to that main object?"[7]

Karl Barth also saw the two viewpoints as providing alternative purposive-explanatory schemes. In Barth's view, the supralapsarian position tells us that

> God had and has a primal and basic purpose which has to be considered and taken into account quite apart from all His other purposes, and therefore quite apart from His purpose to create the world and quite apart from the further purpose to permit the fall of

6. Richard A. Muller, *Christ and the Decree: Christology and Predestination in Reformed Theology from Calvin to Perkins* (Durham, N.C.: The Labyrinth Press, 1986), p. 182.

7. Herman Hoeksema, *Reformed Dogmatics* (Grand Rapids, Mich.: Reformed Free Publishing Association, 1966), p. 164.

man. The original and proper purpose of God consists simply in this: that He Himself, and His glory, and more particularly His mercy and justice, should be revealed among men and to men by means of the salvation of some and the damnation of others. To this proper divine will and decree of God everything else that God wills is subordinate, as an interrelated means to its accomplishment.[8]

Infralapsarianism, on the other hand, is less precise in its account. Barth observes that while it too insists that "God's eternal purpose is to reveal and glorify Himself," it doesn't provide details regarding the content of this claim, refusing to claim "any exact knowledge either of the content of God's primal and basic plan or of the reasons for the divine decree in respect of creation and the fall."[9]

A third objection to the debate focuses specifically on the moral content of the issues that are discussed. David Hume provides a blunt statement of the moral objection in a lengthy endnote to his *Natural History of Religion,* where he appeals to the authority of "the Chevalier Ramsay," who was, Hume assures us, "surely no enemy to Christianity," but who nonetheless expressed considerable outrage at the basic themes of Calvinism: "The grosser pagans," he quotes Ramsay as saying, "contented themselves with divinizing lust, incest, and adultery; but the predestinarian doctors have divinized cruelty, wrath, fury, vengeance, and all the blackest vices."[10] This same objection was spelled out in considerable detail (and with many rhetorical flourishes) by William Ellery Channing, in his 1820 essay, "The Moral Argument Against Calvinism." Calvinism is a religion, Channing argued, whose God does things "from which our moral

---

8. Barth, *Church Dogmatics* II/2, p. 128.
9. Barth, *Church Dogmatics* II/2, p. 129.
10. David Hume, *Principal Writings on Religion: Including Dialogues Concerning Natural Religion and The Natural History of Religion,* ed. J. C. A. Gaskin (New York: Oxford University Press, 1993), pp. 191-92; quote from Ramsay's *Philosophical Principles and Revealed Religion* (Glasgow, 1748-49), Part II, p. 401.

convictions and benevolent sentiments shrink with horror, and which made our pattern, would convert us into monsters!"[11]

A direct response to this moral objection would have to proceed along at least two lines. The first would deal in detail with the basic questions of theodicy being raised. The second would explore the very real possibility that while the alleged moral defects show up very clearly in Calvinism, the same patterns of thought are at least implicit in any theological perspective that takes the full details of the biblical narrative seriously. On this second point, for example, Thomas E. Jenkins has suggested that Channing, in substituting a specific focus on Jesus' example and teachings for the alleged crudities of Calvinism, simply transfers the problem to a different arena — for, as Jenkins points out, many of the character traits that Channing found defective in the Calvinist depiction of God actually show up also in the Gospels' portrayal of Jesus. Channing can make his case, then, only by making selective use of the synoptic materials.[12]

There is also, however, an indirect approach to take in dealing with this, as well the other, objections, which I will pursue in what follows. My focus in this discussion will be on what I see as some more basic issues that are at stake in the infralapsarian versus supralapsarian debate as well as in criticisms that are lodged against the framework in which those debates occur. The issues have to do with how God's character is depicted, how the divine "glory" is to be construed, the status of created reality in general, and the implications of the infra- and supra- positions for how we are to understand our humanness.

11. William Ellery Channing, "The Moral Argument Against Calvinism," in *William Ellery Channing: Selected Writings,* ed. David Robinson (New York: Paulist Press, 1985), p. 118.

12. Thomas E. Jenkins, *The Character of God: Recovering the Literary Power of American Protestantism* (New York: Oxford University Press, 1997), p. 101.

The Divine Character

In his recent study of how American Protestant theologians have understood God's character, Thomas Jenkins observes that the Bible presents us with a God who is characterized by "emotional complexity."[13] The theologians whom Jenkins discusses, however, seem reluctant to give this complexity its due. Instead they look for ways to simplify God's psychic life, usually by appealing to neoclassical, sentimental, or romanticist models of emotional well-being.

The infra- versus supra- debate can be seen, in part at least, as an argument about God's psychic complexity. Both views do, of course, begin with a formal acknowledgement of one overriding divine motive: God is guided in the most fundamental sense by a desire to be "glorified." The supralapsarian position quickly identifies the project by which God chooses to have this desire satisfied: by bringing elect and reprobate human beings to their respective destinies. This state of affairs — which is what God aims at in the most basic sense — is achieved, then, by the decision to create a world and to permit the lapse into sin.

The infralapsarian view insists on more complexity in its treatment of the content of God's self-glorifying designs. God's desire for self-glorification, in the infralapsarian narrative, establishes a broader plot at the outset. The primal decision is to create a world inhabited by human beings, a project that necessitates, for reasons known only to God, allowing sin to come into the picture. This development in turn sets the stage for the selection of a subset of fallen humanity for redemption, with the rest of humankind being allowed to continue in their state of rebellion. While both positions, then, take it as a given that God's fundamental "ruling passion" is self-glorification, each moves in a different direction in its understanding of how God's creating and redeeming designs are meant to instantiate this basic project of self-glorification.

13. Jenkins, *Character of God,* p. 203.

What are we to make of their differing ways of depicting the divine character? Herman Bavinck clarifies the differences by noting that the supralapsarians "subsume all the other decrees under predestination," while infralapsarianism "emphasizes the manyness . . . of the decree."[14] There are at least two grounds to which supralapsarians appeal in rejecting decretal "manyness." One is the doctrine of divine simplicity, which in Hoeksema's thought, for example, means that, since the "counsel of God is one," any attempt to treat providence and predestination as distinct decrees is misleading.[15] The second is the insistence that the divine psyche is exclusively preoccupied — with respect to the end-state of "being glorified" that God's plans are designed to promote — with the eternal status of conscious beings. In Hoeksema's words, "in the counsel of God all other things in heaven and on earth are designed as means to the realization of both election and reprobation, and therefore, of the glory of Christ and His church."[16]

Let us be very clear about what is being said here: if we ask a supralapsarian a question about anything that happens in the universe, the full and correct answer should always be articulated in terms of the eternal destinies of the elect and the reprobate. Why did Plato write *The Republic*? So that the decrees of election and reprobation might be actualized. Why did Babe Ruth hit sixty home runs in one season? Why did President Kennedy approve the plan for the Bay of Pigs invasion? Why did the Tokyo stock exchange experience serious declines during 1998? In every case the answer is that the ultimate point of these events is to promote the realization of God's decision regarding elect and reprobate human beings.

Infralapsarianism, on the other hand, in allowing for an ultimate multiplicity in the divine purposes, is open to a plurality of answers to such questions. There is no reason why, for example, an

14. Herman Bavinck, *The Doctrine of God,* trans. William Hendriksen (Grand Rapids: Eerdmans, 1951), p. 385.

15. Hoeksema, *Reformed Dogmatics,* p. 159.

16. Hoeksema, *Reformed Dogmatics,* p. 165.

infralapsarian could not view God as taking delight in a display of athletic prowess because of ultimate purposes that stand along side of, rather than being subservient to, the goal of bringing about election and reprobation. This is clearly Bavinck's view. Quoting Twissus, he insists that "[t]he different elements of the decree do not stand to one another in a relation merely of subordination, but they are coordinately related."[17] For Bavinck, this allows us to hold "that the [divine] decrees are as rich in content as the entire history of the universe, for the latter is the unfoldment of the former."[18]

God's "Glory"

How are we to understand the references to the divine "glory" as they show up so frequently in these discussions? In some formulations of the supralapsarian case, the God who seeks to be glorified in the decrees of election and reprobation is depicted as a completely self-absorbed being. Hoeksema, for example, sees God as "the One that is Self-centered and is consecrated to Himself, [who] seeks and finds Himself in love. God is attracted by Himself, and He is graciously disposed to Himself. He is charmed by His own loveliness. He delights in His own infinite beauty."[19] This means that God's seemingly other-directed states of consciousness are in fact contemplations of his own self-contained being. The satisfaction that God experiences in the final glorified state of the elect, as a case in point, is in fact a delight in his own holiness; since the church achieves its holiness only in Christ, both the subject and object of God's contemplation of the holiness of the elect are, properly understood, located within the life of the divine Trinity.[20]

There are some interesting parallels here to the efforts of psy-

17. Bavinck, *Doctrine of God,* p. 391.
18. Bavinck, *Doctrine of God,* p. 387.
19. Hoeksema, *Reformed Dogmatics,* p. 112.
20. Cf. Hoeksema, *Reformed Dogmatics,* pp. 126-27, 614-15.

chological egoists to explain all human motivations in terms of every agent's desire to promote his or her own self-interest. To cite some oft-discussed examples, the kamikaze pilot who commits patriotic suicide as an act of devotion to emperor, or the mother who risks her life to rescue her child from a burning building — each of these seemingly other-directed acts is construed by psychological egoism as self-directed. In some important sense, the argument goes, the pilot and the mother are driven by a desire to promote their own individual well-being. Perhaps they expect an eternal reward, or they gain satisfaction while performing the act from the thought of the post-mortem acclaim that will be heaped upon their memory.

Needless to say, from a Reformed perspective, the kinds of objections that can be lodged against psychological egoism as a general theory of *human* motivation do not apply when adapted as an account of the divine psyche. God has every right in the universe to think exclusively in terms of divine self-interest. So, if recognition of God's basic desire for self-glorification turns out to be best understood in terms of God's complete self-absorption, so be it. But whether or not it does turn out this way needs further discussion. At the very least, any notion of a thoroughgoing divine self-absorption must be qualified by an acknowledgement of God's triune being. If we take each of the three persons of the Trinity to be eternally committed to the well-being of the other two, then any talk of a divine "self"-absorption has to be seen as a somewhat misleading piece of shorthand.

But there are other avenues to be explored here as well. The picture of divine self-absorption that dominates, say, Hoeksema's account of God's self-glorifying designs relies heavily on the motif of self-contemplation: God finds himself attractive, God delights in his own beauty, and so on. Herman Bavinck, on the other hand, employs more other-directed imagery in his depiction of God's self-glorifying desires. Having observed that "the manifestation of all God's excellencies is the final goal of all of the ways of God," Bavinck urges us not to think that this ultimate manifestation of God's virtues somehow *consists* in having the elect and reprobate reach their final destinies. Rather, the final state of individuals is just "one of the means employed in order to reveal God's excellencies in a manner suited to the creature." As a way of reinforcing his emphasis on the complexity of God's revealing designs, Bavinck also warns us not to assume

> that in the eternal state of the reprobate God reveals his justice *exclusively,* and that in the eternal state of the elect he manifests his mercy *exclusively.* Also in the church, purchased with the blood of the Son, God's justice is revealed; and also in the place of perdition there are degrees of punishment and sparks of divine mercy.[21]

Again, for Bavinck, God's self-glorifying activity is more than self-contemplation; it includes an other-directed pedagogical motivation: "The idea of the universe was by God so conceived that it is able to reveal his glory and to show forth his excellencies in a manner suited to the creature. . . . [I]t is a finite, limited, inadequate, yet true and faithful reproduction of God's self-knowledge."[22] In such a view, God does not use created reality merely as a dim mirror in which God can discern a reflected splendor; it is also an arena for the display of those excellencies for the creation's own benefit. Bavinck waxes eloquent in his account of this display:

> The "state of glory" will be rich and glorious beyond all description. We expect a new heaven, a new earth, a new humanity, a renewed universe, a constantly progressing and undisturbed unfoldment. Creation and fall, Adam and Christ, nature and grace, faith and unbelief, election and reprobation — all together and each in its own way — are so many factors, acting not only subsequently to but also in coordination with one another, collaborating with a view to that exalted state of glory. Indeed, even the universe as it now exists together with its history, constitutes a continuous revelation of God's virtues. It is not only a means toward a higher and richer revelation

21. Bavinck, *Doctrine of God,* p. 387.
22. Bavinck, *Doctrine of God,* p. 371.

that is still future, but it has value in itself. It will continue to exert its influence also in the coming dispensation, and it will continue to furnish material for the exaltation and glorification of God by a redeemed humanity.[23]

Theology of Creation

It is precisely the range and complexity of this supposed creaturely benefit that preoccupies Karl Barth in his marvelously lucid account of the differences between the traditional infra- and supra- positions. Barth makes it clear that his sympathies are with the supralapsarians — even though he eventually rejects some key assumptions that are taken for granted by both sides. In treating the decree of providence as prior to that of election, Barth argues, the infralapsarians claim that they can discern "in the works of creation and providence . . . a certain general goodness and power and wisdom of God which corresponds to the specific mercy and justice of God in the work of salvation."[24] Barth finds traces in this perspective of the Thomistic insistence that predestination must be seen as a part of providence; he insists that it can only contribute to a watering down of our understanding of election, leading in turn to an endorsement of natural theology. Indeed, it was this tendency, he argues, that weakened Reformed theology's ability "to resist the Enlightenment at the beginning of the eighteenth century, since it carried within it the seed of theological Enlightenment and its own dissolution."[25]

Since Barth recorded these observations several decades before the intellectual community began to proclaim "the failure of the Enlightenment project," it is interesting to compare Barth's historical

---

23. Bavinck, *Doctrine of God,* pp. 392-93.
24. Barth, *Church Dogmatics* II/2, p. 136.
25. Barth, *Church Dogmatics* II/2, pp. 143-44.

claims with "post-Enlightenment" accounts. Alasdair MacIntyre, for example, would agree with Barth that Reformed theology contributed to the emergence of Enlightenment thought, but he places the blame at a very different point. While Barth thought that Calvinists, by separating the decrees of redemption and creation, reinforced the natural theology tendencies that gave rise to a trust in autonomous rationality, MacIntyre complains that Calvinism helped to prepare the way for the Enlightenment precisely because it abandoned what MacIntyre sees as the genius of Thomism. Calvin and his followers, according to MacIntyre's reading of Reformation thought, insisted that we obey the divine commandments out of sheer submission to God's inscrutable will, and not because — as Aquinas and others had taught — those directives promote a generally discernible human *telos*. It was this abandonment by Christian thinkers of a rationally defined conception of human flourishing that encouraged the secularist propagation of the idea of autonomous reason, which, in MacIntyre's view, would inevitably disintegrate, leaving us with the "naked self" of contemporary nihilism.[26]

It is important to consider whether we must choose between the narratives set forth by Barth and MacIntyre, or whether there is another alternative available. What kind of reconstructive project should Reformed thinkers pursue amidst the spiritual and moral devastation of our "postmodern" landscape? Should we firmly oppose anything that smacks of natural theology? Or is the retrieval of at least some elements of the natural theology tradition a helpful strategy for countering the widespread relativism of our day? These questions have an important bearing on how the Reformed community will position itself in the contemporary dialogue between those

26. Alasdair MacIntyre, *After Virtue: A Study in Moral Theory* (Notre Dame, Ind.: University of Notre Dame Press, 1981), 50-52; see also MacIntyre, *A Short History of Ethics: A History of Moral Philosophy from the Homeric Age to the Twentieth Century* (New York: Macmillan, 1966), pp. 121-27. I discuss MacIntyre's account of Reformation thought at length in Mouw, *The God Who Commands* (Notre Dame, Ind.: University of Notre Dame Press, 1990), pp. 55-75.

who insist that we cannot abandon any Christian particularities as we address policy issues in the public square and those who advocate that we employ, whenever possible, a mode of public discourse with broader appeal to citizens of a variety of religious and non-religious persuasions.

These are important matters to pursue, and the considerations that shape our strategies will not be far removed from those that loom large in the debates between infralapsarians and supralapsarians. It is important to ask, for example, why Barth is so convinced that treating creation and election as separate decrees — in the sense that neither is seen as a mere means to the realization of the other — will inevitably weaken our understanding of election. Why, for example, could we not just as plausibly argue that the refusal to distinguish between the two decrees typically leads to a lamentable reduction of available theological resources for dealing with the important issues of public life?

To be sure, a contemporary Reformed appropriation of natural theological emphases will need to proceed more cautiously than did the kinds of medieval accounts to which John Calvin objected. Calvin carefully avoided treating our "natural" religious-cognitive capacities as if they are something that people simply "have" in some static sense. While unbelieving thinkers can offer "competent and apt statements about God here and there," he writes, they always do so with "a certain giddy imagination." The pagan philosopher's awareness of God's purposes, says Calvin, is like that of "a traveler passing through a field at night who in a momentary lightning flash sees far and wide, but the sight vanishes so swiftly that he is plunged again into the darkness of the night before he can take even a step."[27] Calvin's observation is important for us, even though we may want to depict the relationship — or at least the ratio — between light and darkness somewhat differently (Calvin was reacting to

27. John Calvin, *Institutes of the Christian Religion,* trans. Ford Lewis Battles, ed. John T. McNeill (Philadelphia: Westminster Press, 1960), II.2.18.

Christian thinkers who made too much of the light). When we are told that our only choice is either to celebrate the darkness or to curse it, we would do well to think more deeply about a perspective in which lightning flashes provide giddy travelers in the night with occasional glimpses of long-forgotten pathways.

Is Barth right in insisting that by entertaining these thoughts we will weaken our grasp of God's electing purposes? Whether we think so is connected to how we view God's own ability to pursue separate decretal programs. If God cannot operate with more than one "ruling passion," then it would indeed be folly for Christians to attempt to do so; but if God is committed both to the election of individuals to eternal life and to a distinguishable program of providential dealings with the broader creation, then it is quite fitting for us to feature a similar multiplicity in our own theologies.

Understanding Humanness

It is not fair to Barth, however, to address his views on the relationship of creation to election without also acknowledging his own proposed solution to the problems raised in the traditional infralapsarian versus supralapsarian debates. He rejects the notion that the objects of the decrees of election and reprobation are "individual descendents of Adam"; the redemptive work of Jesus Christ should not be viewed, he insists, as the means by which the two groups of human beings are brought to their respective destinies. If we are willing to detach supralapsarianism from this traditional framework, we are then free to see Jesus Christ as *the* object of the decrees of election and reprobation, for he is the one, Barth insists, in whom God has spoken both No and Yes to all humankind.[28] This is an intriguing proposal, because it goes a long way toward remedying traditional supralapsarianism's inability to address matters of ge-

28. Barth, *Church Dogmatics* II/2, pp. 133, 140-41.

neric human concern. Since all of humankind is included in both the Yes and the No that was addressed to Christ, we are free to see the problems of human beings *as such* as encompassed within the scope of God's redeeming purposes.

My own qualms about this proposed solution have to do primarily with my conviction that Barth subordinates the election of individuals to the election of Jesus Christ[29] in ways that do not comport well with the full scope of biblical teachings. The kinds of misgivings that I have on this score have been spelled out in detail by others, including theorists who have considerable sympathy for much of what Barth says in this general area.[30] I will limit my own focus here to some of the underlying concerns that Barth expresses in making his case.

Barth's concerns are two-fold: first, he worries about the focus in the traditional debates on the destinies of distinct human individuals; and second, he dissents from infralapsarianism's emphasis on a created humanness that can be understood apart from redemption. In formulating his first concern, Barth claims to see the threat of "anthropologism" lurking just beneath the surface in the traditional formulations of both supralapsarianism and infralapsarianism. The vulnerability of infralapsarians lies in their insistence that, since creation and providence are independent of the program of redemption, individuals have a certain dignity apart from the decrees of election and reprobation. But Barth sees supralapsarians as even more susceptible to an individualistic fixation, because they view the whole plan of creation and fall as directed toward the single goal of bringing individuals to their eternal destinies. This means, he insists, that for supralapsarianism, "individuals x and y are made the measure and centre of all things to a degree which could hardly be surpassed."[31] Barth even suggests that it is more than a mere coinci-

29. Barth, *Church Dogmatics* II/2, pp. 3-506.

30. See, e.g., Paul Jewett, *Election and Predestination* (Grand Rapids: Eerdmans, 1985).

31. Barth, *Church Dogmatics* II/2, p. 137.

dence that some supralapsarians have been Cartesians.[32] Presumably he means to be drawing a parallel here between Descartes' depiction of the individual consciousness as the testing ground for all truth claims and an understanding of the Christian life in which the experiences of the individual self are placed at the center of things. According to Barth, because the traditional supralapsarian view depicts God as engaged in a "holy self-seeking," thereby finding God's own glory in the electing and reprobating of human individuals, there is a danger that Christians will be caught up in a parallel holy self-seeking, in which they see God as "God for man's sake."[33]

One obvious corrective strategy for the supralapsarian, of course, would be to acknowledge the danger associated with a stress on human individuality and to establish safeguards against it. If God is engaged in holy self-seeking, so be it; our task is to avoid any tendency toward imitating God in this pursuit. As C. S. Lewis suggests in his essay "The Weight of Glory," the best way to avoid thinking too much about one's own glory is not to deny the notion of the glory of individuals as such, but to concentrate on someone else's glory. "It may be possible," says Lewis, "for each to think too much of his own potential glory hereafter," but "it is hardly possible for him to think too often or too deeply about that of his neighbour. The load, or weight, or burden of my neighbour's glory should be laid daily on my back, a load so heavy that only humility can carry it."[34]

Barth's second concern, about a generic created humanness, is especially directed to the traditional infralapsarians, who, he says,

> knew of another secret of God side by side with the decree of predestination. Theoretically at least, then, they knew of another secret of man apart from the fact that he is either elect or reprobate. For them man was also (and indeed primarily) the creature of God, and

32. Barth, *Church Dogmatics* II/2, p. 137.
33. Barth, *Church Dogmatics* II/2, p. 136.
34. C. S. Lewis, *The Weight of Glory and Other Addresses* (Grand Rapids: Eerdmans, 1965), p. 14.

as such responsible to God. This view involved a softening in the understanding of God which is both dangerous and doubtful.[35]

Here too, those of us whose views are being criticized by Barth should not deny the seriousness of the danger he is pointing to; instead, we should acknowledge it and work to establish safeguards. At the same time, however, we need to point to the dangers that attend the *abandonment* of the "secret" about an independently understood created humanness. To make the case from personal experience: I have been acutely aware of these dangers as I have taught and written about ethical and cultural topics in the environs of traditional Calvinism. One topic that has been high on my own agenda is the application of classical just war theory to the violent patterns of contemporary life. On the face of it, a project of this sort should not be difficult for a traditional Calvinist to promote. After all, John Calvin himself regularly articulated the just war perspective, and often with considerable eloquence. At one point in the *Institutes,* for example, he urges magistrates who are contemplating the use of violence to engage in careful self-examination: "let them not be carried away," he warns, "with headlong anger, or be seized with hatred, or burn with implacable severity." Rather, he writes (appealing to Augustine's authority), they must "have pity on the common nature in the one whose special fault they are punishing."[36]

While this is a key passage for teaching just war theory to Calvinists, I have often detected puzzlement when traditional Reformed Christians are confronted with Calvin's point here. How does it square with other important Calvinist beliefs? After all, isn't the human race divided into two classes of people, elect and reprobate? Why then are we so concerned to "have pity on the common nature" that we share with them when God looks at them with full knowledge of the very different — and *un*common — destinies of these two classes?

One way to respond to these concerns is to work within the

35. Barth, *Church Dogmatics* II/2, p. 137.
36. Calvin, *Institutes,* II.8.51.

framework of classical supralapsarianism: we are not God; we do not operate with a clear sense of who is elect or reprobate. So the supralapsarian position at least implies that we need to proceed with an awareness of our finitude. Vengeance is the Lord's business. Our task is to treat even apparent reprobates as potentially elect people of God. This is a coherent line of thought, but I do not find it ethically attractive, because it takes it for granted that the only proper objects of our good will are those persons whom we do not know to be reprobate. The subtext of the argument is that if we *could* know for sure that a person is designated by God as a reprobate, we would have good reason to view that person as not deserving anything more in this life than perhaps a temporary reprieve from a full measure of eternal wrath.

In contrast, Barth's revised supralapsarianism obviously allows for a more positive assessment of our enemies. Since God has addressed both a No and a Yes to them in Jesus Christ, we can fulfill Calvin's requirement that we presuppose a "common human nature" with our enemies while still viewing them (in good supralapsarian fashion) within the categories of election and reprobation. But for those of us who are not convinced by Barth's rationale for his revisionist view, our only option is to emphasize the bonds that hold within a common created humanity — what the Canons of Dort refer to as that "whole human race" whose status in God's plan is not governed solely by the redemptive program. For me at least, this perspective provides a helpful and necessary Reformed framework for dealing with the issues of war and peace, as well as other urgent human matters.

Social Embodiments

It is not uncommon for commentators on the differences between supra- and infralapsarians, having come down on one side of the dispute, to acknowledge that the other position nonetheless poses a helpful reminder of something important. Let me also offer such a concession. While my own sympathies are clearly with the infralapsarians in their understanding of God and God's dealings with created reality, I must confess that I find it spiritually profitable to wrestle with the picture set forth by supralapsarians. As a Calvinist, I need to be reminded that my own moral or aesthetic objections are never sufficient for refusing seriously to consider the starker depictions associated with supralapsarian views.

In his recent book exploring the kinds of spirituality associated with wilderness landscapes, Belden Lane quotes the theological complaint of the lapsed vicar in John Updike's novel *A Month of Sundays*. Tired of a "limp-wristed theology" that appropriates psychological themes in order to cater to the needs of a generation of self-actualizers, the Rev. Thomas Marshfield pleads, "Let us have it in its original stony jars or not at all!" Lane finds something compelling about this manifesto. "Why does such a harsh and unmeasured Connecticut-Calvinist outburst," he asks, "strike within us a deep prophetic chord? In a society that emphasizes the limitless possibilities of the individual self, it comes as a strange freshness to be confronted by an unfathomable God, indifferent to the petty, self-conscious needs that consume us."[37]

Lane's personal confession captures something of my own theological mood when dealing with the topics I have been discussing; yet in the final analysis, I find that I am also deeply affected by what I see to be the social embodiments of the infralapsarian and supralapsarian positions. Alasdair MacIntyre makes the intriguing suggestion that every "moral philosophy . . . characteristically presupposes a sociology," such that "we have not yet fully understood the claims of any moral philosophy until we have spelled out what its social embodiment would be like."[38] In a similar vein, I propose

---

37. Belden C. Lane, *The Solace of Fierce Landscapes: Exploring Desert and Mountain Spirituality* (New York: Oxford University Press, 1998), p. 53.

38. MacIntyre, *After Virtue*, p. 22.

that every theological system also has an associated sociology, such that we can fully understand the claims of a theological perspective only if we attempt to see what it would look like if those claims were fleshed out in the life of a community. Thus an examination of such a link can be used to test cautiously the adequacy of the theological position in question. What kinds of sermons would be preached? What would be the patterns of spiritual formation? How would ecclesial decisions be made? How would spouses treat each other, and how would they raise their children? What would be the character of the community's evangelism, counseling, and catechizing? How would the members of the community deal with the pressing problems of humankind in general? With respect to this last question, I sometimes allow my imagination to wander into even broader territories. I think about what it would be like for Stanford University to establish a professorship of international economics in the name of Theodore Kreps — and to stipulate that the chair must be occupied by an infralapsarian!

Chapter Five

SEEKING THE COMMON GOOD

In 1992 I published a book on the topic of Christian civility.[1] I wrote it because I was concerned about the fact that, in a world where incivility rules the day, the words, actions, and attitudes of Christians often make the problem worse. As a modest contribution to a remedy for this unfortunate state of affairs, I offered a biblically grounded case for Christian civility, albeit a rather "generic" Christian one. Drawing on some key biblical themes, I wanted to provide Christians, especially evangelical Christians, with reasons to exhibit and promote civility. I will not rehearse the details of that discussion here, but I do want briefly to describe the basic pattern of my overall case, in order to set the stage for exploring connections between those more "generic" considerations and the more confessionally specific themes of Calvinist thought.

1. Richard J. Mouw, *Uncommon Decency: Christian Civility in an Uncivil World* (Downers Grove, Ill.: InterVarsity Press, 1992).

Two Principles

The case for Christian civility, as I see it, requires that we establish two important principles. The first is that Christians must actively work for the well-being of the larger societies in which we have been providentially placed. And the second is that sanctified living should manifest those subjective attitudes and dispositions — those virtues, if you wish — that will motivate us in our efforts to promote societal health.

The Bible, as I see it, provides us with a strong basis for each of these principles. I find I Peter 2:11-17 to be one of the richer teaching passages with regard to both of them. The apostle urges believers to "conduct yourselves honorably among the Gentiles," while accepting "for the Lord's sake the authority of every human institution" (vv. 12-13). The obligation to manifest honorable conduct does not mean, however, that believers should do whatever will *please* everyone in the larger society; indeed, fellow citizens might well "malign you as evildoers." The important thing is to act in such a way that unbelievers "may see your honorable deeds and glorify God when he comes to judge" (v. 12).

Peter establishes the context for these instructions at the beginning of his epistle when he salutes this particular group of New Testament believers as "the exiles of the Dispersion" (1:1), an allusion repeated in the reference in 2:11 to Christians as "aliens and exiles" — a motif that is further reinforced by the use in 2:9 of four titles previously applied to Old Testament Israel ("a chosen race, a royal priesthood, a holy nation, God's own people"). This allows us to draw a fairly direct parallel to the instructions, recorded in Jeremiah 29, that the Lord gave to the newly exiled people of Israel. Having been wrenched away from their theocratic context in Jerusalem, the exiles were now wondering how they were to conduct themselves in Babylon. So the prophet gives them their new instructions for exiled living: they are to construct dwellings for themselves, and plant crops for their sustenance (v. 5); they are also to enter into marriages, and to encourage their sons and daughters to do likewise, so that they all might bear children and increase their numbers in the land (v. 6). And then this important mandate: "But seek the welfare *(shalom)* of the city where I have sent you into exile, and pray to the Lord on its behalf, for in its welfare *(shalom)* you will find your welfare *(shalom)*" (v. 7).

In all of this, of course, the children of Israel are to maintain a strong sense of their own identity as God's elect people. And the same holds for the citizens of the New Israel. The apostle Peter insists that the exiled Christian community must "abstain from the desires of the flesh that wage war against the soul" (2:11). And in spelling out, in 2:17, the four obligations of their life as the New Israel, he chooses verbs that highlight their primary identity. They are to "fear *(phobeo)* God" above all, and "love *(agapao)* the family of believers"; then in describing what they owe both to the emperor and to their fellow citizens in the larger society he uses the same verb twice — "honor *(timao)*."

This "honoring" of — having regard for the well-being of — other human beings is at the heart of Christian civility. It is the same subjective disposition that Peter urges us to cultivate in a different formulation later on in his first epistle: "Always be ready to make your defense to anyone who demands from you an accounting for the hope that is in you," he tells us; "yet do it," he adds, "with gentleness and reverence" (3:15-16).

In my book I made rather quick work of connecting this counsel to the *imitatio dei*. I argued that in our efforts to cultivate gentleness and reverence toward all human beings, to honor them, we should see ourselves as imitating some of God's own traits. In saying this, I was conscious of the fact that as a Calvinist I was moving a bit fast over this theological territory; I went out of my way to acknowledge that I did not mean to deny the "harsher" dimensions of the Bible's portrayal of the divine character. God's "sovereignty, holiness, power, wrath and the like" are very real, I insisted, and I had no desire "to 'tame' the God of the Bible."[2] But then I quickly

2. Mouw, *Uncommon Decency,* p. 35.

moved on to stress the gentler dimensions of God's dealings with humankind.

In this context, however, I will try to pay my Calvinist dues on the subject, for at least two reasons. One is simply a matter of confessional integrity — I want to be able to demonstrate that my "generic" Christian case for civility can indeed be grounded in Calvinist thought. The other pertains to ecumenism: the theological issues at stake here have taken on new ecumenical significance in recent years, and Calvinists should make their theological contribution to the larger discussion. Indeed, I am convinced that it is good for Calvinists to "go public" with many of the arguments — such as the common grace debates — that we have typically carried on only among ourselves.

A Vow of Abstinence?

How are we to understand in specifically Calvinist terms the mandate to seek the *shalom,* the common good, of the larger societies in which the Lord has placed us in the time of our exile? Some Calvinists have made a case for refraining from active promotion of the common good, not because they think that pious withdrawal from the larger culture is the norm for the Christian community, but because they believe that sinful conditions are such that voluntary abstinence from such activities is the only plausible communal strategy. This is the position advocated by Klaas Schilder, who is certainly aware of the emphasis in the Calvinist tradition on the cultural mandate. Schilder has harsh words for that kind of "Christian [cultural] abstinence" that "originates in resentment, laziness, diffidence, slackness, or narrow-mindedness"; such, he says, "is sin before God." But there is also a "heroic" abstinence, and this is what he espouses. This brand of cultural abstinence is at work when "Christian people [are] maintaining their colleges, supporting their missionaries, and caring for the needy who were left them by Christ, . . . [and] are doing a thousand other works of divine obligation" that make it difficult for them to perform those highly visible works of "cultural transformation" that Kuyper and others urge upon the Christian community. This abstinence does not deny the legitimacy of a broader cultural calling, but "because of the emergency situation" it "finds its limits and legitimation in, e.g., Matthew 19:12, where Christ speaks about those 'that make themselves eunuchs for the Kingdom of heaven's sake' and not in order to avoid this Kingdom."[3] This self-limiting pattern is not simply anti-culture, but it does restrict the territory in which we carry out our cultural activity.

There is something to be said for this vow-of-abstinence approach to cultural involvement. Schilder is certainly right to insist that the seemingly modest acts of obedience that are directed to the "internal" strengthening of the life of the church can be important acts of cultural faithfulness. One of the significant cultural tasks that the Christian community must perform in the world is simply to *be* a community — a fellowship of people who, in the patterns of their life together, serve as a sign of faithfulness in the larger world. Schilder makes an important point when he observes that the wise church elder who faithfully visits his assigned congregational members "is a *cultural force*, although he may not be aware of it."[4] And it may even be quite legitimate for a specific Calvinist community — or an Anabaptist one, for that matter (since I suspect that many Anabaptists do precisely the kind of thing that Schilder recommends) — to limit its cultural tasks to these seemingly modest patterns. Just as individuals have specific callings, so do particular Christian communities. For example, one legitimate way to think positively about the fact of multiple Christian denominations may be to see different denominational groups as having different vocations — different assignments from the Lord to work out different virtues and to cultivate different

---

3. Klaas Schilder, *Christ and Culture*, trans. G. van Rongen and W. Helder (Winnipeg: Premier Printing Ltd., 1977), pp. 69-70.
4. Schilder, *Christ and Culture*, p. 86.

spiritual sensitivities. Schilder's use of the "eunuchs for the sake of the Kingdom" image would be quite appropriate to this approach. One Christian community might take a vow to abstain from that which another Christian group might actively pursue.

This would not satisfy Schilder, of course; he would require from *all* Christian churches a vow of cultural abstinence. Such a far-reaching claim requires critical scrutiny. What is it about our present world that requires this pattern of abstinence? It is clear, for example, that the Lord called his people in Old Testament times to work for the well-being of the larger Babylonian society in which he had placed them during their time of exile. Was the cultural "emergency" less serious in those times? Is there something unique about our contemporary situation that requires all of us to be cultural eunuchs? Schilder's wartime experiences of hiding for months at a time from the Nazis, for example, might have led him to think of "emergency" measures. But why should his specific recommendations apply under present cultural conditions to the whole Christian community, or even to the whole *Calvinist* community?

Agents of Common Grace

For those who do not feel called to cultural abstinence, it is important to consider the notion, which I introduced in the previous chapter, of *common grace ministries*. The standard formulations of common grace teaching have often had an unfortunate feel of passivity for Christians. They have depicted a transaction between God and unbelievers with virtually no attention to the active role of the Christian community in "delivering the goods," so to speak, of common grace.

The Christian Reformed Church's Three Points of 1924 certainly seem designed to encourage cultural passivity. They come across as instructions for Christians who are mere observers of the larger world. Of course, we cannot help being largely passive when it comes to the "natural blessings" — such as sunshine and rain — that are bestowed upon the elect and non-elect alike. But the second and third areas are different. We should not just stand back and watch for signs that God is restraining sin in the world, or hope that we might witness acts of civic righteousness popping up here and there in the lives of the unredeemed. We ought to look for ways God can use us to restrain the power of sin in the larger human community, and to perform our own works of civic good. Calvin's views on the magistracy reflect this needed sense of activity. "No one ought to doubt," he writes, "that civil authority is a calling, not only holy and lawful before God, but also the most sacred and by far the most honorable of all callings in the whole life of mortal men."[5] And unlike the Anabaptists, he was convinced that Christians themselves can perform this noble calling.

But common grace ministries are not restricted to the political realm. Abraham Kuyper pointed to broader areas of service when he referred to the Christian obligation "to continually expand the dominance of nobler and purer ideals in civil society by the courageous action of its members *in every area of life.*"[6] The Christian psychologist who encourages her non-Christian clients to honor commitments, the Christian literature professor at a secular university who highlights themes in a novel that celebrate faithfulness and telling the truth, the Christian corporate manager who instills the will to serve in employees, the Christian farmer who employs specific agricultural methods that demonstrate respect for the integrity of the creation — all of these promote the goodness associated with common grace. We should not confine our attention, then, to how unbelievers on occasion perform those deeds that better the lot of other human beings. We should also think about the ways in which we

5. John Calvin, *Institutes of the Christian Religion,* trans. Ford Lewis Battles, ed. John T. McNeill (Philadelphia: Westminster Press, 1960), IV.20.4, p. 1490.

6. Abraham Kuyper, "Common Grace," in James D. Bratt, ed., *Abraham Kuyper: A Centennial Reader* (Grand Rapids: Eerdmans, 1998), p. 197; emphasis mine.

ourselves, in performing righteous acts that affect the lives of unbelievers, can promote the gifts of common grace.

Of course, a rationale could be conceived for some of these activities that has nothing to do with common grace. Suppose, for example, we insist that Christians have an obligation to take up the cause of the poor — not only those Christian poor whose plight was mentioned by Schilder in his advocacy of cultural abstinence, but the poor in general. One could hold that we ought to do this simply because God *commands* us to do so. And one could hold, further, that these commands are purely salvific in what they aim at — that God wants us to promote the cause of the poor because mixed in among them are some of the elect, and that while we may not be able to discern the difference between elect and reprobate poor, we can be sure that by promoting the cause of the poor in general we are also bettering the lot of the elect poor, the ones whom God *really* cares about. Such a rationale could constitute a legitimate basis for a supralapsarian political activism. It is not a view I would endorse, but when it comes to Calvinist advocacy for the poor, we should take whatever we can get!

Nevertheless, I do not think such a view is theologically adequate, because it does not require us to care about the non-Christian poor. And I believe we are commanded to care for *all* those in poverty. Furthermore, I am convinced that in cultivating that kind of caring disposition we are imitating *God's* concern for all impoverished people. Which is to say that a proper theology of poverty, and more broadly, of justice, is inextricably linked to common grace — the teaching that God has a positive, albeit non-salvific, regard for those who are not elect, a regard that he asks us to cultivate in our own souls.

Calvinist Empathy

The opponent of common grace will, of course, insist that we seriously misunderstand God's intentions in all of this. All of the non-elect, says Herman Hoeksema, are the enemies of God, and God "hates His enemies and purposes to destroy them, except them He chose in Christ Jesus."[7] This does not seem to comport well, however, with Christ's command to "love your enemies, and do good, expecting nothing in return" even as the Father "is kind to the ungrateful and the wicked" (Luke 6:35). When the Savior refers here to people who curse us and abuse us, is he thinking exclusively of our *Christian* enemies? It seems unlikely. In any event, John Calvin apparently did not have such a restricted understanding of which enemies merit our concern. When magistrates think about going to war, he writes, not only should they take great care "not to be carried away with headlong anger, or be seized with hatred, or burn with implacable severity," but they should also "have pity on the common nature in the one whose special fault they are punishing."[8]

If this "pity on the common nature" is an appropriate attitude to cultivate toward an "armed robber," as Calvin says here, should we not be even more diligent in cultivating kindness toward those who are victims of various sorts of oppression? The bishops at Vatican II put it well, I suggest, when they began their "Pastoral Constitution on the Church in the Modern World" *(Gaudium et Spes)* with these words: "The joy and hope, the grief and anguish of the men of our time, especially those who are poor or afflicted in any way, are the joy and hope, the grief and anguish of the followers of Christ as well. Nothing that is genuinely human fails to find an echo in their hearts."[9]

We Calvinists should consider ourselves to be operating under this kind of empathy mandate as well. The Christian therapist was

---

7. Herman Hoeksema, *The Protestant Reformed Churches in America: Their Origin, Early History and Doctrine* (Grand Rapids: First Protestant Reformed Church, 1936), p. 317.

8. Calvin, *Institutes*, IV.20.12, p. 1500.

9. *Gaudium Spes* ("Pastoral Constitution on the Church in the Modern World"), in Austin P. Flannery, ed., *Documents of Vatican II* (Grand Rapids: Eerdmans, 1975), p. 903.

right to weep with the non-Christian couple reaching out to one another in a newfound tenderness. We are right to react with horror to what happened to the Muslim mother whose unspeakably cruel experience I described in a previous chapter. But we must not simply allow these affective responses passively to "happen to us." We ought actively to *promote* "the joy and hope" and to *diminish* "the grief and anguish" of our fellow human beings, regardless of their election or reprobation.

"Thick" and "Thin" Speaking

Actively promoting the welfare, the shalom, of the larger human community will require us also to speak in the public square about policies and practices that can restrain sin and even contribute to positive patterns of civic righteousness. Here too — perhaps *especially* here — the questions about commonalties are important. What language shall we employ when we talk with our fellow citizens about the issues of public life? Do we speak the "thick" discourse of our own confessional particularity, and risk being misunderstood or ignored? Or is it legitimate to translate the terms we use among ourselves into a "thin" public discourse that relies upon less specifically Calvinist or even Christian language, to make the case for our policy proposals in a way that might convince someone who does not share our theological convictions?

Some of the "post-liberal" mainline Protestant thinkers mentioned earlier have been quite critical of the Christian use of "thin" public discourse. Stanley Hauerwas, for one, has insisted that Christian ethics must be grounded in the practices of a highly particularized Christian community whose moral discourse is radically discontinuous with that of the larger culture. Such a vision is reflected in the title of one of his books: *After Christendom? How the Church Is to Behave If Freedom, Justice, and a Christian Nation Are Bad Ideas.* Of course, Hauerwas does not reject the idea of justice as such, but he does worry that Christian presumptions of an available common moral discourse signal that we have negotiated an unfaithful compromise with the fallen order.[10]

A more nuanced perspective has been set forth by the Roman Catholic ethicist Bryan Hehir, a primary advisor to the United States bishops on matters of public policy. He acknowledges that he has been deeply influenced by the natural law tradition, and has long operated on the assumption "that when speaking to the state, the church must use a language the state can comprehend." While he still basically adheres to this position, he has come to see its limits as well: "in surveying the principally social policy debates of the 1990s," he writes, "I am also struck by the limits of the ethical, that is to say the failure of the purely moral argument to address the underlying dimensions of our public policy disputes and decisions." He believes it is important for us to attend especially to "the premoral convictions that must be addressed to confront the societal questions we face today." And on these matters, he says, "the comparative advantage is with communities that are convinced of the kind of theological truths the Christian community takes for granted. These are embedded convictions — capable of being articulated, so not unintelligible for public discourse." What this means in practice, Hehir suggests, is that we are severely limited in our use of theological language "when we finally address the state on law and policy . . . but prior to stating the policy issue we can and should expansively engage the wider civil community in the deeper questions that undergird policy choices, and that may take theological argument to surface, because they are about our basic relationships as a society and a human community."[11]

---

10. Stanley Hauerwas, *After Christendom? How the Church Is to Behave If Freedom, Justice, and a Christian Nation Are Bad Ideas* (Nashville: Abingdon Press, 1991).

11. J. Bryan Hehir, "Personal Faith, the Public Church, and the Role of Theology," *Harvard Divinity Bulletin* 26, no. 1 (1996): 5.

Calvinist Messiness

In good Catholic fashion, Hehir makes much of the incarnation in providing the theological rationale for his understanding of the public role of the Christian community. Not only has God appeared in human history in the person of Jesus Christ, but this incarnational event is extended "in time and space," so that God continues to "touch and transform" human reality — a process to which the church bears witness as it "carries the transforming grace of Christ in history."[12]

This is not the way we Calvinists would want to make our point. Reformed thought operates with a less expansive understanding of the incarnation. As the Heidelberg Catechism puts it, Christ is not "according to his human nature . . . now . . . upon earth," for he has taken our flesh to heaven with him as the ascended Lord, and it is from there that he presently reigns over all things "according to his Godhead, majesty, grace, and Spirit."[13] Therefore, while we, like Hehir, want to speak with our fellow citizens about the fundamental questions of the human condition, our motivation is not that we think an incarnational transformation of humanity is occurring beyond the boundaries of the church. Instead, we remind ourselves that the world at large is still afflicted by the cursedness of the fall. To repeat: we do not make our witness in the larger world on the assumption that humankind has been made more receptive to the truth of the gospel by some kind of across-the-board upgrade. We proceed with caution, knowing that the rebellious manifesto of our first parents — "We shall be as gods!" — still echoes all around us. But we also know — and this is an important message for common grace theology — that the Spirit of the reigning Lamb is indeed active in our world, not only in gathering the company of the redeemed

---

12. Hehir, "Personal Faith," p. 5.

13. Heidelberg Catechism, Questions and Answers 47, 49, in Philip Schaff, ed., *The Creeds of Christendom, with a History and Critical Notes,* vol. III (Grand Rapids: Baker Books, 1996), pp. 322-23.

from the tribes and nations of the earth, but also in working mysteriously to restrain sin in the lives of those who continue in their rebellion, and even in stimulating works of righteousness in surprising places. And so, while we proceed with caution, we also go about our business in hope.

Admittedly, there is a large measure of messiness in the picture I have just drawn. As Calvinists, we must seek the common good with the clear awareness that in the public square we are surrounded by people "who call good evil and evil good, who put darkness for light and light for darkness, who put bitter for sweet and sweet for bitter" (Isaiah 5:20). And yet it is in these circumstances that we hear again the Lord's ancient call to his redeemed people to seek the welfare of the city of our exile. This messiness, then, isn't something that we can hope to eliminate; nor can we minimize it as we develop our strategies for public witness. To endorse a common grace theology is to learn to live with some theological messiness. This ought not to trouble Calvinists, for whom the experience of theological messiness should be a healthy reminder of the ways in which all of our theological probings will eventually bring us to a humble acknowledgement of the divine mysteries.

Messiness will also attend our efforts to sort through the merits of "thick" and "thin" language as we engage in our public discourse. What we say when we are addressing the issues of public life, and how and when we say it, are questions that can be answered only by a continuing reliance on discernment. That in turn means that we must be deeply rooted in the community of God's redeemed people, where the Lord has promised to distribute the gifts of his Spirit as we wrestle together with the challenges of public discipleship. And it is there that we are constantly reminded of our promise of a pattern of community far better than the public square as we now know it. Even as we seize the public opportunities available to us during this time of the Lord's patience with a rebellious world, we yearn for "a city that has foundations, whose architect and builder is God" (Hebrews 11:10).

In his wonderful essay "On Secular Authority," Martin Luther warns that the Christian prince must be spiritually vigilant if he wants to guarantee that "his condition will be outwardly and inwardly right, pleasing to God and men." And in doing so, Luther quickly adds, the prince "must anticipate a great deal of envy and suffering," for it is inevitable that he "will soon feel the cross lying on his neck."[14] Luther's words are true not only for princes, but for all of us who hear the call to work as Christians for the common good of the larger human community. When our Calvinist ancestors lived under conditions of severe persecution, they knew that their only recourse was to immerse themselves in a community shaped by the preaching of the Word, the administration of the sacraments, and the exercise of discipline, even when doing so was a risk to their very lives. In such circumstances, they chose to describe themselves as "the churches under the cross." The truth of the matter is that there is no other place for Calvinists of any age to make their primary abode. And when we do venture forth to serve the Lord in the broader reaches of human culture — as I am convinced we must — it is good to anticipate that we too will inevitably feel the cross lying on our necks.

14. Martin Luther, "On Secular Authority," in Harro Hopfl, ed., *Luther and Calvin on Secular Authority*, Cambridge Texts in the History of Political Thought (Cambridge: Cambridge University Press, 1991), p. 41.

Chapter Six

UPDATING COMMON GRACE THEOLOGY

E arly on in this discussion, I endorsed the verdict of theologian Foppe Ten Hoor, who confessed in the 1920s that after forty years of thinking about common grace he was fairly sure that there is such a thing, but he really did not have a very good idea of what it is. Ten Hoor made good sense. Indeed, the spirit of his comment about common grace ought to be given freer play in other areas of theological debate. As Thomas Weinandy has recently observed, theology is best understood as "a mystery discerning enterprise" rather than "a problem solving" one. To solve a problem is to make all of our puzzles go away, which is not the kind of resolution that we ought to expect as a matter of course in theological exploration. But we can hope to succeed in knowing "more precisely and clearly what the mystery is" — and this can be an important gain.[1]

I have tried to discern here some of the contours of the mystery of common grace. I am quite aware of the fact that I have only touched briefly on topics about which much more needs to be said. Perhaps what I have said here will revive a discussion of a topic that

---

1. Thomas G. Weinandy, O.F.M., Cap., *Does God Suffer?* (Notre Dame: University of Notre Dame Press, 2000), pp. 32-34.

has received little attention in recent years on the part of main-stream Reformed theologians. Yet it should be obvious from what I have said thus far that I do not think that it is sufficient for us simply to remember some important lessons from the past when we think about common grace; we must also update our understanding of it. And as I bring this discussion to an end, I want to highlight some important aspects of this updating, as well as some key cautionary concerns that ought to guide it.

Assessing Alternatives

Properly understood, common grace theology is an attempt to preserve an area of mystery regarding God's dealings with humankind. In an important sense, an acknowledgement of common grace is arrived at by a "way of negation"; it is something we are left with after having gone through a process of elimination. Calvinists have typically been unable to endorse with much enthusiasm any of the other major efforts in the Christian tradition to formulate an understanding of what it is that Christians and non-Christians have in common. Outside of the Calvinist tradition, the major alternative views — general revelation, natural law, and natural theology, for example — have commanded considerable respect and been put to extensive use in establishing patterns of commonality. But we Calvinists have generally approached these explanatory schemes with many misgivings.

Not that we have been inclined simply to reject the core ideas associated with each of them. That would be misguided — especially, I would suggest, in our contemporary cultural context. God has indeed lawfully ordered his creation, and there are biblical passages — Romans 2:15 is an obvious case in point — that make it clear that all human beings have some sort of cognitive access to that lawfulness. The same sorts of things can be said about general revelation. Does God reveal something of his person and attributes through means other than biblical revelation? Of course. The Belgic Confession states clearly that in addition to God's revelation in Scripture, "[w]e know him . . . by the creation, preservation, and government of the universe; which is before our eyes as a most elegant book, wherein all creatures, great and small, are as so many characters leading us to contemplate *the invisible things of God,* namely, *his eternal power and Godhead*" — all of which is "sufficient to convince men, and leave them without excuse."[2]

But Calvinists typically refuse simply to take such things for granted, in the sense that we can assume that all human beings have "automatic" access to the cognitive and motivational resources necessary for doing good things for the right reasons. Even in interpreting the statement that I have just quoted from Article II of the Belgic Confession, many Calvinists have insisted that we cannot take at face value what appear at first glance to be some unambiguous claims about common access to truths about God. For example, they have asked, who are the "we" who are said to gain knowledge of God from the book of creation? Isn't the reference to "knowing" here limited to those in whom sovereign grace has worked to open the eyes of faith? And aren't those others referred to in this article, those unbelievers who are "without excuse" because of what is manifestly revealed in creation, are they not actually being condemned for *not* seeing that which *would* have been very plain to them if they had not rebelled against God?[3]

In a passage that I pointed to earlier, the Canons of Dort capture this Calvinist ambivalence succinctly in describing the effects of the fall on human consciousness. While the unregenerate do retain "the

2. Belgic Confession, Art. II, in Philip Schaff, ed., *The Creeds of Christendom, with a History and Critical Notes,* vol. III (Grand Rapids: Baker Books, 1996), p. 384.

3. For an extensive discussion of these matters, see G. C. Berkouwer, *General Revelation; Studies in Dogmatics* (Grand Rapids: Eerdmans, 1955), especially Chapter 10, "The Controversy Regarding Article II of the Belgic Confession." For a succinct account of the Protestant Reformed understanding of Article II, see Herman Hanko, *For Thy Truth's Sake: A Doctrinal History of the Protestant Reformed Churches* (Grandville, Mich.: Reformed Free Publishing Association, 2000), pp. 141-57.

glimmerings of natural light" that provide them with "some knowledge of God, of natural things, and of the difference between good and evil," the Canons say, not only is this awareness wholly inadequate for bringing people to salvation, but the fallen person is actually "incapable of using it aright even in things natural and civil. Nay farther, this light, such as it is, man in various ways renders wholly polluted, and holds it [back] in unrighteousness; by doing which he becomes inexcusable before God."[4]

A Continuing Caution

Needless to say, Christians from other traditions will find it strange that Calvinists are so nervous about such matters. And rightly so, for there are some important differences at stake here. I think the main concern for Calvinists about general revelation, natural law, natural theology, and similar notions is that they can lead to a categorical endorsement of the moral and rational capacities of human beings in general. Either the radical effects of the fall are denied outright, or they are acknowledged and then quickly modified by the idea of a prevenient grace, an across-the-board upgrading of our original fallen state, so that some significant segment of our shared human consciousness has been repaired and our depravity is no longer in effect. Henry Van Til describes the resulting theological perspective with an allusion to World War II stories about American soldiers sharing cigarettes with their German enemies on Christmas Eve: "there is between the church and the world a grey, colorless area, a kind of no man's land, where an armistice obtains and one can hobnob with the enemy with impunity in a relaxed Christmas spirit, smoking the common weed."[5]

4. Canons of Dort, Heads III and IV, Art. IV, in Schaff, *Creeds*, Vol. III, p. 588.

5. Henry R. Van Til, *The Calvinistic Concept of Culture* (Grand Rapids: Baker Book House, 1959), p. 240.

While Calvinists often say some positive things about the moral and intellectual accomplishments of the unregenerate, we are nervous about giving the impression that there is something *carte blanche* about these assessments, or something "automatic" about the unregenerate person's ability to think good thoughts or to perform laudable deeds. As a result, common grace teaching encourages more of an ad hoc approach to evaluating the moral and intellectual capacities of the unregenerate. To employ the idea properly in assessing the thoughts and deeds of the unconverted is to operate with what we might think of as a hermeneutic of caution, though not a hermeneutic of outright suspicion. For we do not want to miss those splendid encounters that John Calvin assures us will come our way — and which he warns us not to misinterpret, lest we "dishonor the Spirit of God" — those occasions where "the mind of man, though fallen and perverted from its wholeness, is nevertheless clothed and ornamented with God's excellent gifts."[6] Nor is it, in the other direction, a hermeneutic of solidarity, in which we *presume* truth and goodness. We must proceed with caution, not wanting to miss the true and the good, but realizing that not all that glitters is the kind of ornamentation John Calvin wanted us to see.

Still, this is an important time for Calvinists to be taking an honest look at our traditional spirit of caution regarding common grace. At the very least, we need to be clear about how much of our arguing with other Christian traditions about the moral and cognitive abilities of the unredeemed has been motivated by a polemical spirit. Calvinist theologians have been a rather testy lot. We have wanted to keep the boundaries clear between our own perspectives and those of Anabaptists, Catholics, Lutherans, and others. Much of this keeping of boundaries makes sense in the light of a variety of historical factors. But we now live in a different age, one often enam-

6. John Calvin, *Institutes of the Christian Religion,* ed. John T. McNeill, trans. Ford Lewis Battles (Philadelphia: Westminster Press, 1960), II.2.15, pp. 273-75.

ored with nihilism and relativism, such that it should be very clear to all of us in the Christian community that we need to explore the rich dimensions of the gospel together. In this context, we need to search collectively through a variety of traditional theological resources for addressing contemporary ills. Common grace teaching is one such resource, but natural law theory and the theology of general revelation also have a great deal of relevance to our present-day situation. Contemporary challenges present us with a good opportunity for a broad-ranging, friendly discussion of these various theological resources.

Fragmented Psyches

I am also convinced that the way we address these issues ought to be more consciously linked to practical concerns about promoting — as much as possible in our fallen world — conditions for human flourishing. My own worries in this area run rather deep these days. To be sure, this concern about how to promote human flourishing in our contemporary context has to do with issues that range far beyond the territory covered by common grace theology as such. But the notion of "commonness" is at the core of what I worry about.

The commonness topic was raised for me in a poignant manner a few years ago by a brief comment from a person who called into a radio talk show. I was a guest on this particular program, and I was paired with another theologian in a discussion about the continuing fascination in our culture with the person of Jesus of Nazareth, as evidenced in frequent cover stories in weekly newsmagazines, TV specials, and the like. My fellow guest, a very liberal Protestant, expressed some strong skepticism about the reliability of the New Testament accounts of the resurrection of Jesus — an assessment with which I strongly disagreed. When we opened the discussion to questions from our listening audience, one of our callers was a teenager who identified herself as Heather from Glendale. Heather expressed herself in typical "Valley Girl" tones: "I'm not what you would call, like, a Christian," she began. "Actually, right now I am sort of into — you know — like, witchcraft and stuff. But I want to say that I agree with the guy from Fuller Seminary. I'm just shocked that someone would, like, say that Jesus wasn't really raised from the dead!"

I was taken aback by Heather's way of offering support for my position. Her comment still strikes me as rather bizarre — combining a fascination with "witchcraft and stuff" with a belief in the literal resurrection of Jesus. And the more I have thought about what Heather said, the more I worry about her and what she represents in our contemporary culture.

To be sure, I can imagine having an enjoyable conversation with Heather. In the account given in Acts 17, the Apostle Paul was engaged in what looked like a productive and friendly dialogue with some Athenian philosophers, until he told them about the resurrection of Jesus; then many of them began to ridicule him. But the narrator adds: "others said, 'We will hear you again about this'" (Acts 17:32). Some of these latter folks, we are told, eventually became believers. I have often wondered what the conversation was like when Paul talked further to these pagan inquirers who were intrigued by the idea of Jesus' resurrection. Maybe a conversation with Heather from Glendale would give me a feel for the tone of that dialogue.

Nevertheless, I worry about Heather. I am concerned about the way she seems to be piecing together a set of convictions to guide her life. While I did not have the opportunity to quiz her about the way in which she makes room in her psyche for an endorsement of both witchcraft and the Gospel's resurrection narratives, I doubt that Heather subscribes to both views of reality, Wicca and Christianity, in their robust versions. She is placing fragments of worldviews side by side without thinking about their relationships. And it is precisely the fact that these disconnected cognitive bits coexist in her consciousness that causes my concern.

What increases my worrying is that there are intellectual leaders who actually celebrate this kind of disconnected selfhood. Take the case of Kenneth Gergen, a psychologist who has written a much-discussed study of contemporary selfhood entitled *The Saturated Self: Dilemmas of Identity in Contemporary Life*. There Gergen argues that traditional conceptions of how to understand personhood — whether or not people have souls or unconscious minds, their "intrinsic worth" or "inherent rationality" — have been exposed by "the postmodern turn" as inappropriate:

> These are, after all, ways of talking, not reflections of the actual nature of persons. In contrast to the narrow range of options and the oppressive restraints favored by totalizing systems of understanding, postmodernism opens the way to the full expression of all discourses, to a free play of discourses.[7]

In this way of viewing things we help people best, says Gergen, by inviting them into an "endless wandering in the maze of meaning," in which they regularly experience "the breaking down of oppositions."[8] To be sure, Gergen wants individuals to find some way of blending various "richly elaborated discourses into new forms of serious games that can take us beyond text and into life."[9] But it is not clear exactly what standards are to guide this process in a world in which all comparative judgments are arbitrary, indeed "imperialistic." Why should my Dodger-fan self have any less status in my life than the self that senses a need to serve the poor? Why should I prefer any instinct or preference to any other one? In such a world, what is the difference between a healthy and an unhealthy self? What would keep each of us from proclaiming, like the young demoniac whom Jesus encountered, "My name is Legion; for we are many" (Mark 5:9)?

---

7. Kenneth J. Gergen, *The Saturated Self: Dilemmas of Identity in Contemporary Life* (New York: Basic Books, 1991), p. 247.

8. Gergen, *Saturated Self*, p. 256.

9. Gergen, *Saturated Self*, p. 259.

A Larger Fragmentation

My worries about the landscape of Heather's inner life extend also to the broader scene, the larger moral and spiritual context that has contributed to her psychic confusion. There is a sense in which Heather is a microcosm — or a micro-chaos — of the larger culture.

Back in 1990, *Harper's* magazine invited five specialists on urban life to discuss what is and is not happening in America's public spaces today. The editors asked the experts particularly to address the decline of public life that is resulting in the "debauched public discourse" of talk radio and Jerry Springer–type TV shows (actually, in those days the prime example was "Geraldo"). The assembled experts included two architects, one urban planner, a sociologist, and a sculptor, so they naturally paid special attention to the physical dimensions of urban life. And while the experts did not agree among themselves about how best to construct a healthy public space, they were unanimous in thinking that things are not going well in our urban communities. Nor were they confident that better urban planning alone would solve the problems. As one of the architects put it, "What we long for in the design of our public space and in the character of our public life is not fragmentation and difference but a sense of what we have in common while knowing our difference — a sense of wholeness."[10]

My Calvinist convictions do not allow much optimism about finding significant "wholeness" in either our private or our public lives without the transforming power of redeeming grace. But neither can I give up completely on the possibility that we can still witness in our contemporary milieu some evidences of the workings of common grace as an integrating and preserving power. Nor can I give up on the possibility that active Christian involvement in common grace ministries can *promote* those evidences.

10. Elizabeth Plater-Zyberk, "Whatever Became of the Public Square?" *Harper's*, July 1990, p. 60.

Signs of Hope

I want the Christian community to explore the meaning of human commonness as it applies to the real-life situations of Heather and others like her. And the theology of common grace, with its underlying assumption of a substantive humanness that we all share, gives me hope in taking up that exploration. It also inspires me to look for signs of an awareness of that commonness, even in places where the notion of a shared humanness seems to have been thoroughly "deconstructed."

Kenneth Gergen suggests that we think of the intermingling of our diverse discourses as a "carnival" of sorts, which would allow us to introduce an element of *playfulness* into our internal and external conversations; but I prefer a broad-ranging conversation that gets beyond playing on the surfaces and probes the deep places in our ways of experiencing reality. Roman Catholic philosopher Albert Borgmann, who has analyzed the ways in which the postmodern consciousness often limits its attention to the *surfaces* of reality, supports the possibility of this kind of conversation. He addresses this malady with a call to rediscover the deeper dimensions of reality in its rich particularity, to recognize "the things that command our respect and grace our life."[11] What theologian Mark Heim has said about the proper character of interreligious dialogue applies even more broadly to the larger pluralistic conversation in public life: "the better we know [other] faiths from the inside, the better we will sense where in a deep sense we can affirm them and where in our dialogue we must speak critically, as we are willing to listen."[12] I am convinced that if we listen carefully, we will be able to discern, even in the confusion of tongues that plagues the lives of Heather from Glendale and others like her, deep yearnings that arise out of a shared humanness.

11. Albert Borgmann, *Crossing the Postmodern Divide* (Chicago: University of Chicago Press, 1992), p. 82.
12. S. Mark Heim, *Is Christ the Only Way? Christian Faith in a Pluralistic World* (Valley Forge, Pa.: Judson Press, 1985), p. 150.

A few years ago, Jacques Derrida became embroiled in a controversy over the publication of one of his essays in a volume published
by Columbia University Press. Derrida did not like the translation —
or the translator — and took legal action to keep the volume from
appearing. *The New York Review of Books* gave considerable space to
the charges and countercharges, labeling the dispute "L'Affaire
Derrida." At one point in the exchange, Derrida expressed considerable frustration over his critics' allegations. He regretted having to
respond again, he said, but it was necessary nonetheless "to recall a
few stubborn and massive facts" that should not be ignored.[13]

This is one of a few times that I have taken delight in something
written by Derrida. His formulation here — "a few stubborn and
massive facts" — is intriguing, and worthy of broader application.
There is good reason to keep the conversation going with those
postmodern thinkers who profess to be interested only in surface
minglings of "multiple discourses." The signs of deeper yearnings
for commonality and consensus are there to be seen, if we are willing
to pursue the conversation. Those of us who care about establishing
a more adequate basis for civil society than seems available in the
present "carnival" must insist that our fellow citizens face up to "a
few stubborn and massive facts" about human nature. If we are per-
sistent, we may find new occasions for discovering together an eloquence that can be discerned only in the deeper places of our individual and collective lives.

A Wide Mercy

Throughout this discussion I have been rather free in employing the
well-worn Calvinist categories of "elect" and "non-elect" or "reprobate." I make no apologies for doing so. The categories are biblical

13. Jacques Derrida, letter in "'L'Affaire Derrida': Another Exchange," *The
New York Review of Books,* March 25, 1993, p. 65.

ones. Nevertheless, I do not mean to mean to imply that I actually
have clear notions about how to divide the human race up into these
classifications. Here too — even *especially* here, I am convinced — we
mortals stand before a great mystery. But I do want to make it clear
that while I am no universalist, my own inclination is to emphasize
the "wideness in God's mercy" rather than the "small number of the
elect" motif that has often dominated the Calvinist outlook. I take
seriously the Bible's vision of the final gathering-in of the elect, of
that "great multitude that no one could count, from every nation,
from all tribes and peoples and languages," who shout the victory
cry, "Salvation belongs to our God who is seated on the throne, and
to the Lamb" (Revelation 7:9-10). For all I know — and for all any of
us can know — much of what we now think of as common grace may
in the end time be revealed to be saving grace. But in the meantime,
we are obligated to serve the Lord in accordance to patterns that he
has made clear to us. Calvinists have rightly been fond of quoting
Deuteronomy 29:29: "The secret things belong to the Lord our God,
but the revealed things belong to us and to our children forever, to
observe all the words of this law."

What we must keep in mind, however, is that "all the words"
God has spoken to us include also words of compassion for human
beings who live in rebellion against the divine ordinances. In Calvinist thought, the need for exercising this compassion has been
grounded in a strong theological emphasis on the fact that all human beings are created in the divine image. At their best, Calvinists
have insisted that God himself continues to cherish that which he
has created, even when that created reality has become deeply dis-
torted by sin. "So does God miss every soul that falls away from
Him," says Abraham Kuyper, because the effect of our sin is "to spoil
the work that God has made, and to wound Him in the likeness of
Himself." As Kuyper saw it, the sinful assault on our humanness "is
as though you took a child, and before the eyes of his mother struck
him down, and maimed him for life. It is to defy the love of the
Maker for His handiwork, willfully giving offense, and grieving the

Maker in that about which His heart is most sensitive."[14] If God's deep love for humanity persists even despite the effects of sin, then the theology of common grace is an important resource for our efforts as Christians to respect and reflect that love.

14. Abraham Kuyper, *To Be Near Unto God,* trans. John Hendrick De Vries (Grand Rapids: Baker Book House, 1979), pp. 30-31.

3 6877 00182 6329

BT
761.3
.M68
2001

DATE DUE